3

MONTE AMIATA

With a gentle, but nevertheless imposing outline, visible also from afar, Monte Amiata creates a solemn background to Sant'Antimo as it emerges like a final rampart of the Tuscan land, before encountering the province of Lazio. With a height of 1,738 m., it dominates over the Orcia valley at the North (Montalcino, Pienza, Montepulciano); over the Sienese hills at the East (Chiusi, Chianciano, the Chianti zone); and over the great expanse of the South-West Maremma area.

Luxuriant beech-wood forests, rocks with exceptionally odd forms, mines, abundant spring water (also thermal) and particular types of flora – 40 different species of orchids - have all remained unaltered, and can still be appreciated by one who is in search of cool and shade during the summer. And also by those who, from the months of December to March wish to frequent one of the most complete skiing complexes of the Tuscan province.

The Fauna Park of Monte Amiata, situated on the slopes of Monte Labro, is considered to have the darkest amongst sky zones on account of the complete absence of light pollution, and houses stargazers from all over the Italian peninsula - in search of limpid skies.

Inf.: www. webamiata.it

MONTALCINO

Inf.: www.prolocomontalcino.it

① As a rule, one arrives at Sant'Antimo passing through Montalcino. Whether arriving from the north or from the south, along the Cassia, Montalcino appears in front of you, at a distance, high up, with its wide outstretched profile, interrupted every now and again by towers and belfries. Amidst olive trees and vineyards, it dominates over those valleys found to the east of the river Asso, to the west of the river Ombrone, and to the south of the river Orcia. The volcanic profile of Monte Amiata closes the southern horizon of this little town in the province of Siena.

The residence of the Priors and the public diocesan museum, with paintings by Simone Martini, Pietro Lorenzetti, and other Tuscan artists, as well as an

Montalcino

It's a beautiful summer's day. I have just left Siena, and am driving southwards. Big cities, traffic, noise, the usual encounters, or tagging along to art monuments greyed over with pollution, have no appeal to me… I know that in the district of Siena there are tiny little worlds to explore - villages, churches, estates, farms, abbeys and castles still well preserved. I allow my eyes to guide me as I cross the bare clay hills, famous throughout the world for their warm ochre, yellow and green colouring. These areas tell stories - thousands of years old - about princes, counts, bishops and saints, artists and craftsmen, painters and peasants. The rigorous and at the same time simple architecture of these zones have defied the centuries, continuing to our day with its solemn and untouched charm.

From the radio within my car, songs, jokes and phrases continue to burst forth. Today, however, I am seeking some peace. I stop the car to consult the guide. While leafing through the pages, the photo of a church in Romanesque style, isolated and beautiful, attracts my attention – it's the abbey of Sant'Antimo, about 50 km to the south of Siena. It is there that I decide to go.

I drive along singing happily in anticipation of a new discovery. All at once, in the distance, I notice a white slender figure walking along the side of the road. On approaching closer, his features become ever clearer; it is a religious brother – a religious brother who is hitchhiking! He wears a white tunic and has a becoming smile. I stop the car and ask him, "Father, would you like a lift? Where are you going?"

He replies with a question, "And you?"

"I'm on my way to Sant'Antimo. The abbey of Sant'Antimo."

"Oh how nice! I'm also going there!"

He gets into the car and puts out his hand, "Ciao, I am brother Giovanni, and you, what is your name?"

"Francesco," I reply.

Then the brother adds, "How come that you are going to Sant'Antimo?"

"Because I read in the guide-book that there is a beautiful church, a real masterpiece of art; I want to see it. And then, that a community which celebrates the liturgy in a very old type of singing, the Gregorian Chant, lives there – for quite a few years now. I want to hear it. And hmm… then…there's also good wine there! And you, why are you going to Sant'Antimo?"

The brother fixes his eyes on the road and with a somewhat mischievous smile replies, "Because that is where I live!"

Rather embarrassed, I just keep quiet. In a friendly way brother Giovanni continues, "If you like, I will teach you not only to look and to hear, but also to observe and to listen, and above all, to get to know and to venerate the Abbey of Sant'Antimo. I'll guide you so that you can discover an art treasure which conceals and protects within itself an unexpected and even more precious treasure, the treasure of faith."

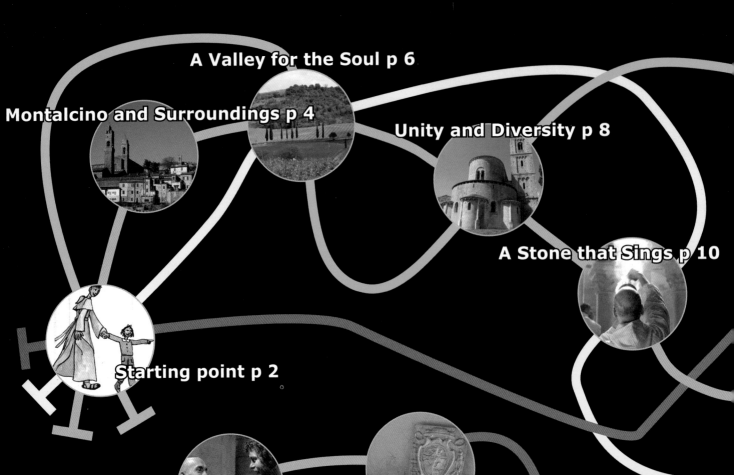

GUIDE TO THE GUIDEBOOK

In order to simplify the reading of the text, we present four itinerar-
ies, each indicated by a different colour:

    the entire itinerary that Francesco (our imaginary visitor)
    made, accompanied by the brother.

    the artistic itinerary at Sant'Antimo.

    the historic itinerary.

    the itinerary relating to the Community and its spirituality.

(the number refers to the page)

important medieval wood-sculpture section are to be found in the old characteristic medieval town centre. The main attraction of this place is however, the Fortress (Fortezza), a huge medieval castle, with a most unusual scenic impact – and a symbol too of Sienese autonomy in opposition to that of Florence. Nowadays it is used as a spectacular stage for plays and concertos, while room has been made in the keep for a wine cellar of great renown. The precious 'Brunello' one of the most famous Italian wines – pride and boast of these regions – can be tasted there.

(2) Following the compulsory roundabout signal at the foot of the fortress, the traffic-sign indicates the road to Castelnuovo dell'Abate and the Abbey of Sant'Antimo. The road winds along following the hillside curves, to present large panoramic views on every turn – now onto the lower-down valley, now on dark and shady ravines thickly overgrown by the Mediterranean shrub.

A mysterious atmosphere and intangible feelings accompany the journey towards this extraordinary and eagerly awaited encounter. All at once, the abbey appears in front of you, there, at your right, centred on a large clearing. You are unable to tear your eyes away from it. You perceive it, it is real, but it sweeps you into the surrealism of a dream – it seems to be a vision. A precious pearl encased amidst the velvet of emerald green plains.

nd Surroundings

THE ORCIA VALLEY

Sant'Antimo is the old centre and heart of the Artistic, Natural and Cultural Park recently founded by the 5 communes of this area: Castiglione d'Orcia, Montalcino, Pienza, Radicofani and San Quirico d'Orcia. To make a visit to this Park means to enter amidst the colours and features of Sienese art in an area that is unique in the whole of Italy, distinguished by certain types of geological earth formations named: 'crete', 'biancane', 'calanchi'.
Inf: www.valdorcia.it

CASTELNUOVO DELL'ABATE

The medieval village of Castelnuovo dell'Abate, found at 395 m. above sea level (Sant'Antimo is found at 318 m. above sea level), is an outlying administrative division belonging to the commune of Montalcino. The town is partly surrounded by old walls with an arch-formed entrance on the southern side, facing the main road. Worth visiting are the bishop's palace and the frescoes in the parish church. About 200 inhabitants make their living by farming (vineyards and olive trees) and sell these products in the town basements. A grocery-shop, a bar, and 2 restaurants (Trattoria Bassomondo: 0577 835619 – Locanda Sant'Antimo: 0577 835615) offer refreshments for tourists. A bus service connects Montalcino to Castelnuovo dell'Abate about four times a day (348.74.08.676).

Inf: www. castelnuovoabate.it

At the foot of the hill on which Castelnuovo dell'Abate is built, on the south-west side, a travertine and alabaster quarry is found. This quarry is very old and for centuries was used for the construction of buildings. The stone was still being drawn out up until the year 1990.

A Valley
for the Soul

I was very fortunate to be present at the Mass on Easter Sunday. A fantastic experience! It was like a breath of fresh air to me in a moment when my life was full of chaos and smog. I should like to convey that emotion to the whole world. I should like that in the whole world peace could reign as it reigns here.

From: "Libro d'oro" at www.antimo.it

Poggio d'Arna

Castelnuovo dell'Abate

Welcome sound, when I heard them sayin

 he Starcia, a tributary of the river Orcia, runs across the little valley where the abbey rises. This valley is framed by the undulating profile of the surrounding hills. Brother Giovanni points towards a hill and says, "At the north you can see a hill called Castellare on which a fortified village had once been built (named 'Castello' in medieval times), and which had then been abandoned for unknown reasons, leaving only a few remaining stones. To the south you can see the actual built-up area of Castelnuovo dell'Abate. To the west, the sunset on the Maremma remains hidden by Poggio d'Arna, where, quite recently, a cross 17 meters high, was planted in honour of Charlemagne. The hills, somewhat lower and with more open space towards the east, are dotted over with rows of cypresses, and crossed by little white country roads. Each morning, as the sun rises behind these hills, slowly, like an unrestrained tidal wave, it floods the ancient stones of this abbey with its golden rays."

Above all, dear brothers, love God and then your neighbour, because these precepts are the most important. The reason for which you are united together is, first and foremost, so that you live unanimously in the house with one heart and one soul only towards God. (Rule)

Villa Tolli

Poggio Castellare

"We will go to the Lord's house." (Psalm 121)

4 I arrive at the bottom of the valley. The steep descent is now more levelled. The abbey is much closer. It invites me to stop in order to admire it. From across the field, the magnificent apse, the bell tower and the cypress create a unique and exceptional sight. I stand still to look at it, and almost feel the need to convey, with a light sweeping touch, all my admiration for the soaring elegance of its lines, the solidity, the magnificence and compactness of its architecture.

5 Only on advancing a little more closely, I notice that one apse, i.e. the first to the left, differs somewhat from the other. It is much smaller, and seems quite older.

Brother Giovanni seems to guess my thoughts, and says, "Yes, that is true. As such it is older than the rest of the building. It is the famous Carolingian apse.

It belongs to the primitive church that was built at the time of Charlemagne."

Primitive church? Carolingian apse? But whatever is this brother talking about? This abbey has a rigorous and uniform aspect, simple and solemn – an unequivocal sign denoting a single architectonic style.

The brother continues, "What you are looking at today is nothing more than the final effect of enlargements and embellishments made around the year 1100, as decided by the Benedictine monks who had been living here since the 8th century. But I don't want to confuse you. I will explain bit by bit. Come with me!"

Unity and Diversity

And he walks off quickly towards the main entrance, keeping close to the north side. I stay behind, because I want to take a photo. I want to have a keepsake when I get home. The brother stops, to indicate a precise spot on the wall of the bell tower where a bas-relief, with a cornucopia dating to the Roman era, can be seen.

At last the façade is in front of us.

CORNOCUPIA

The experts retain that this sculpture in white marble probably came from a Roman villa. At first the cornucopia was thought to be the horn of the goat Amalthea, or of the fluvial god Achelaus that had been broken off by Heracles during a battle. Picked up by the Naiades, it was decorated according to the symbol that it was destined to become. It is the emblem of overabundant fortune and of a very copious harvest. It is said that in the point at which this figure fixes its gaze, a great treasure would be hidden.

A Stone that Sings

(6) The façade seems incomplete. I look about to find some evidence of its primitive splendour, and my eye is caught by an unusual capital which depicts a monster with one head and two bodies, on the top of a column to the left of the entrance. But on the other side of the main door, something attracts my attention ... a sound, or rather, singing, coming from within. It's a choir of men's voices chanting an unknown melody never heard before. Brother Giovanni perceives my amazement and says, "This is a church, the house of God. My brothers are now praying within. They pray with the Gregorian chant, which distinguishes them. Come, and let us too go in, to greet the Lord!"

(7) I look through the doorway, and am stunned by the dazzling wave of lights and sounds that envelop me - while an intangible veil of incense penetrates me overall as in every corner of the church. Beams of light flow down from the windows, to caress the light-coloured stones, the arches, the capitals, the altar, and the church decorations... Then my attention is suddenly arrested - down there - by the luminous and resplendent presbytery lit up by the light of the sun, where some brothers are standing, as they sing on either side of the cross. It's a moment of deep and intense emotion.
Brother Giovanni who is next to me, understands, "It is certainly not so easy to remain indifferent in the midst of so many beautiful things all concentrated in a single place!" And then goes on to whisper, "It is the liturgy of the Eucharist that is being celebrated, and my brothers are now singing the antiphon at the communion. We must not disturb them."

(8) He signs to me to go out. As soon as we are outside, I pester him with questions, "But who are these monks? What are they doing here? When did they come here?"

Well accustomed with always replying to the same questions, he smiles in resignation: "We are neither monks or friars, but a community of Regular Canons. We draw our inspiration from the Premontratensien Order founded by Saint Norbert in the 12th century, and from the Rule of Saint Augustine. To speak briefly, we are priests here who serve the local church, and the diocese... but I don't want to say everything altogether! While we are waiting for the Mass to finish, come with me, and I will show you the more ancient part of this abbey."

SAINT AUGUSTINE ORGANISER OF COMMUNITY LIFE FOR PRIESTS

Saint Augustine is the father of our spirituality. He was born at Tagaste (North Africa) on the 13th November in the year 354. He died in the year 430 at Hippona (Africa) on the 28th August, date on which we now celebrate his feast day.

Brought up according to the Catholic faith, he lived a dissolute life in his youth until the reading of Cicero's "*Hortensius*" drew him back again to the life of the spirit. Attracted by the Manichean heresy, the encounter with Saint Ambrose – by whom he was then baptised – brought him back to the faith. On returning to Africa after his mother's death, he founded a monastery at Tagaste, and then two monasteries of laymen at Hippona, where the *otium sanctum* (absolute contemplation in silence and solitude),was the main occupation.

The great innovation came about when Augustine, a passionate lover of community life, began to live personally with the priests of his diocese - first as a priest and then as Bishop of Hippona, with two basic commitments: community life, and pastoral service. He wrote a Rule that was then used by the communities of the Regular Canons during the 11th century.

Philosopher, theologian, mystic, orator and polemist, to him is attributed the first synthesis between philosophy and faith which demonstrates how a perfect conciliation is possible between the earthly city and the heavenly city. In the world in which we live today, where it seems that the earthly city is in conflict with the heavenly city, his message remains ever yet an admonition and a hope for humanity.

Origin and Foundation

Signature of the Emperor Louis the Pious. Charter dating to the year 814 (A.S.S.)

(9) We have now entered through the gate where once the cloister had stood. I gaze to my left, towards the south wall of the church, where I notice a main door of undoubted artistic value. I get closer in order to admire the beautiful decorations: mythological animals on the architrave with foliage motifs and geometrical designs on the side posts.

Brother Giovanni begins to narrate: "This door belongs to the 10th century. It dates back to the period preceding the erection of the large church. Try to imagine this place in those far off times. We are on the territory conquered and then ruled over by the Lombards…"

I interrupt him, and say, "I remember having read that the abbey of Sant'Antimo was founded by Charlemagne. The court and army of the Frankish king had been struck down by a pestilence in the neighbourhood of Mount Amiata. The emperor begged the help of God for the ceasing of the plague, and having thus obtained the grace, as a sign of gratitude, built this church."

(10) The brother smiles at me, and continues, "There are many people who know the legend which ascribes Charlemagne as the founder of this monastery. You know, in the Middle Ages, it was customary to augment the importance of certain edifices, attributing with extraordinary events the foundation to a celebrated personality. Unfortunately, the tourist guides or other popular texts frequently cite only this data, continually utilising the same sources, without making more accurate historic researches on the matter. And so time passes and … the legend remains. The historic facts, however, differ somewhat. Now I will explain to you what most probably came about, to begin many years before the Carolingian epoch.

(11) "As a matter of fact, the primitive building nucleus is to be traced back to the epoch when the relics of Sant'Antimo of Arezzo were venerated. At the death of the saint, some pious persons built a little chapel over the place of his martyrdom, in order to pray there at his tomb. A Roman villa already existed on the spot, data confirmed by the presence of archaeological findings to be seen in the abbey, such as the bas-relief with the cornucopia, on the north side of the bell tower, or some columns in the Carolingian crypt, dating to the Roman epoch. It is thought that there must also have been a fount with curative qualities, because a fragment of stone was found with the inscription "Venite et bibite". We know that in the year 715 this martyr church dedicated to Sant'Antimo was in the keeping of a priest belonging to the diocese of Chiusi."

N.B. (in order to simplify, and to distinguish it from the subsequent constructions, we will name this first nucleus 'Sant'Antimo 1').

RIVERS, STREAMS AND SPRINGS

The Starcia valley has water in abundance. Besides the Starcia, which flows into the river Orcia, there is also another stream named Colombaiolo that comes down from Villa Tolli. It joins the Starcia at a short distance from the Romanesque bridge next to the old mill of Castelnuovo dell'Abate. Moreover, four water-stratum pass under the church, at a depth that varies from ten to twenty meters. We know too that

water coming down from the Arcangela fountain situated at that point where the slopes of the hill Castellare begins, was conducted to the monastery to finish up in the cloister. Curiously enough, already in the 16th century the water had been conducted into the church, and from a basin on the inside, then poured forth into a sarcophagus, which stood on the north side of the cloister.

12 "Roundabout the year 770, the Lombards designated the Abbot Tao, (of Pistoian origin), to build the first Benedictine monastery (which we will name 'Sant'Antimo II'), entrusting him the administration of the state property of that territory on which the monastery was to be erected. In fact, the Lombard kings utilised the existing monasteries, and frequently they would build new ones at a distance of 30 km between them, in order to establish halting and refreshment posts for the pilgrims on their way to Rome. These posts were also necessary for the merchants, the soldiers, and the king's messengers, passing along that route.

13 "On his return from Rome in the year 781, while keeping to the main route of communications devised by the Lombards (named 'Francigena' because the road was of French origin), Charlemagne arrived at Sant'Antimo. On that occasion, he set his seal on the foundations of this first monastery, then being erected. On the 29th December, 814, a charter of Loius the Pious, son and successor of Charlemagne, enriched the abbey with gifts and privileges. Sant'Antimo therefore became an imperial abbey in every way – an investiture that would serve to move it towards the maximum of it's development."

The brother interrupts the narrative, and has me sit down beside him on a low stone wall, most probably that which now remains of the outer wall of the old cloister.

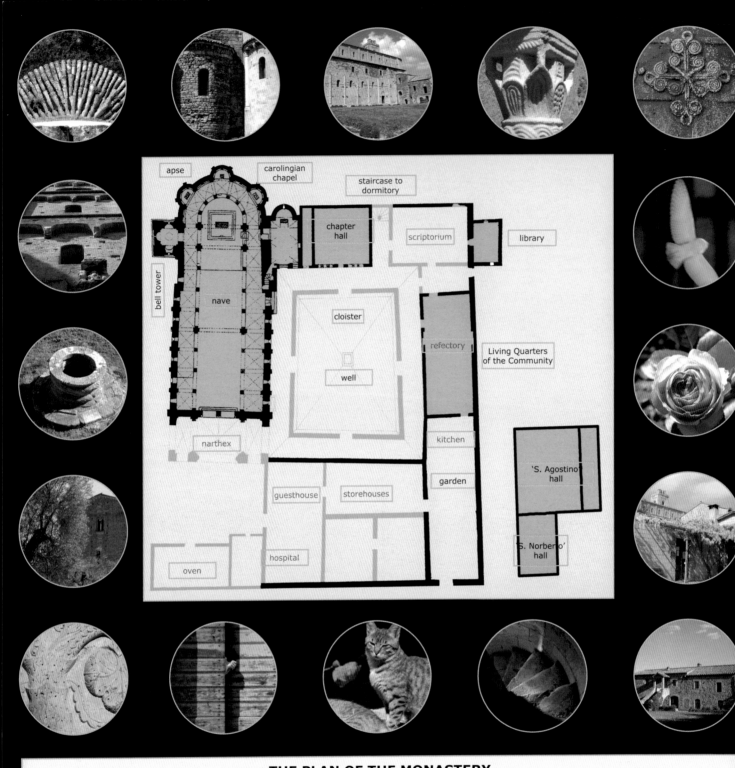

Plan labels: apse · carolingian chapel · staircase to dormitory · bell tower · chapter hall · scriptorium · library · nave · cloister · refectory · Living Quarters of the Community · well · narthex · kitchen · 'S. Agostino' hall · guesthouse · storehouses · garden · hospital · 'S. Norberto' hall · oven

THE PLAN OF THE MONASTERY

Even if they differed in measure, complexity, and use of materials, all the monasteries built by the Benedictines in medieval Europe – in Galicia as in England, in Switzerland as in Burgundy, in Lombardy as in Normandy – had at least one point in common: the plan.

The church, with its apse orientated towards the east according to the liturgical custom, nearly always has a cloister adjoined on the southern side (the old Roman atrium) with a covered gallery or passageway on all four sides.

In the east gallery of the cloister, parting from the church, the sacristy, the treasury, the chapter hall, the staircase leading to the upper floor, and the 'scriptorium' (with a large fireplace), are found. On the upper floor is the monks' dormitory, frequently

connected to the church in order to allow the monks ready access for nocturnal prayer. Along the gallery on the south of the cloister – directly opposite the church - the refectory, often furnished with a fountain, is collocated. The kitchen is situated on the corner where the south wing encounters the west wing, and gives access to the refectory on one side, and to the exterior on the other side. The storehouses and pantries are generally situated on the western side, while the dormitory of the laymen is found on the upper floor. Also rooms for guests or pilgrims, the hospital, the laundry, the bakery, and other buildings – where the monks could work – were built near the monastery.

The actual structure is designed in black, while the hypothetical reconstruction of the destroyed sections are designed in grey.

(14) I look about me. Stones are scattered on the ground and amongst the grass - most probably remains from old collapsed walls. These signs left by time, do not however, detract anything from the awesome beauty of the place.

Brother Giovanni looks at me, and takes up the subject again as he says, "Do you remember how your attention was drawn by the two different apses, when you arrived at Sant'Antimo? Well, from this first abbey of the 7th century, called the Carolingian chapel, that old apse now remains visible on the outer side. Internally it forms a single rectangular nave. The roof, now groin-vaulted, originally must have had simple wooden trusses. Monochrome frescoes by Giovanni d'Asciano (15th century) cover the walls and depict the life of Saint Benedict. It is now used as a sacristy, to which one enters by a door found along the ambulatory on the southern side of the church."

(15) My guide gets up and walks towards an entrance where the steps in front of it go down to a lower level than that of the cloister plane.

"Come," he says, " I want to show you another architectonic masterpiece: the Carolingian crypt! You may consider yourself very fortunate to be able to visit this crypt, because as a norm, the crypt, the sacristy, and the matroneum are not accessible to tourists."

I follow him, as I try to accustom my eyes to the semi-darkness that envelops the little hall. "This underground crypt has two apses exactly opposite each other. One stands on the eastern side, with a little bull's eye to provide some light, and corresponds to that of the upper church, while the other consists in an ordinary semicircular niche, to be found on the western side. Four re-used colonettes surmounted by capitals,

The First Monastery

which are inverted truncated pyramids, support the vault, dividing the space into three tiny naves. In this little crypt, not open to tourists, the brothers still come to pray and to meditate in its idyllic and silent atmosphere."

(16) We leave the crypt, to find ourselves again in the sunlit cloister. Brother Giovanni, raising one arm, calls my attention to what now remains of a beautiful tri-lobed window. "Also this triple lancet window from the 8th century, dates back to the latter period of this abbey. As you can see, one capital is completely unadorned, without any decoration, whereas the other one is decorated with eight palm leaves and a woven geometrical design. This window belongs to the chapter hall."

He stops, and then asks me, "Do you know why the chapter hall bears that name?" I cough a bit, and stare into space.

With a particular expression on his face, the brother decides to help me, and explains, "In his Rule, Saint Benedict admonishes the monks to read daily one chapter of it. As time went by, the hall where a chapter of the Rule was thus read, took on the name of 'chapter' hall. Today all the professed members of the community (also named 'the Chapter') assemble there. It is a characteristic feature of the Regular Canons to keep a daily reunion in the chapter hall, diversifying from the other Orders who meet only occasionally. In the chapter hall, the martyrology is read, followed by the reading of a chapter from the Rule of Saint Augustine, and lastly, information on problems relating to the day's work is then exchanged."

And do not regard anything as belonging to you, but let everything be in common. The superior must provide each one with food and clothing, not on an equal basis to all, because not all of you enjoy the same health – but providing each one according to his personal needs. In the Acts of the Apostles, in fact is said: 'They kept everything in common and to each was given according to his personal needs.' (Rule)

(17) The brother continues the conversation as he points at the southern church wall. "The series of stone corbels on the same level as the architrave – to the left of the portal – served to support the beams that sustained the roof of the cloister gallery, now completely destroyed. Traces of the original foundation suggest that the cloister formed a square, the sides of which were approximately 19 metres long. This very deep cistern at the centre of the courtyard was built in the 16th century on an already existing medieval well. It still receives rainwater just as it did then."

(18) While he's speaking, the door facing the cloister opens, and hastily the brothers file out one by one across the open courtyard which separates the church from their living quarters. On passing by, each one glances at me, to greet me briefly, "Ciao, ciao!"

One of them, with a smiling face, and piercing look, asks me, "Do you like the abbey? Are you one of our guests?"

Not without blushing a bit, I reply, "For the moment, I am only a visitor."

(19) My guide then intervenes: "Today, as yet, all that we do remains connected with this cloister. We cross it about six times a day, in order to go and sing the Liturgy in the church, and for the celebration of the Eucharist. The bell constantly marks and regulates our daily life, as it calls the community to prayer. Now, after the Mass, as you can see, each one of us attends to the work assigned him. One goes off to welcome the Scouts or the tourist pilgrims, another to study, another for pastoral service in a nearby parish, another to do manual labour (i.e. work necessary to maintain the house), and another to answer the numerous telephone calls. Towards 12.45 p.m. all of them will leave their occupations in order to come together for the singing of Sext in the presence of the Lord."

Life is quiet in the cloister...? But these brothers don't stop even for a second!

The brother continues, "Now that the Mass is over, we can visit the church. Come, let us now enter by the main doorway."

The Façade

20 Once more we return in front of the church, and step onto the embankment in front of the main entry. I stop in order to admire the portal somewhat hidden by the branches of the centuries old olive trees growing in front of Sant'Antimo. My friend again continues to explain: "Those semi-pilasters with the attached columns, standing against the façade, and the traces of arches evident on the wall, lead us to believe that the portal must have been preceded by a portico. The architrave dates back to the 12th century. It is sculpted with a foliate vine, which symbolises the Tree of Life. An interesting Latin inscription informs us about Azzo dei Porcari (a family from Lucca) - 'monk, father, and then deacon' - who most probably was the author of the magnificent architectonic innovations brought about in the church, without having been able, nonetheless, to supervise the actual execution. In fact, he died about ten years before the grandiose construction was begun. When I explain

the following part, you will understand more easily what I am talking about.

(21) "The rest of the portal is of a slightly later period. The capitals, the frieze with vegetal motifs, and the recessed fluted arch, all recall the Toulousan prototypes. We will find this French influence in other parts of the church as well. The portal, as it stands today, is probably a make-shift solution. The original project must have been comprised of two portals equal in width to the nave."

My attention is drawn to the frieze on the architrave. "What type of stone was used for the execution of the portal?"

"A local stone, partly travertine, and partly alabaster," replies the brother.

"But travertine is a light-coloured stone, how come this ochre colour?"

"Because in the Middle Ages the external sculptured stones were treated with an ochre-coloured powder mixed together with organic substances derived from fish."

Quite astounded, I ask, "For what purpose?"

"In order to protect the stonework from the wearing action of time. Quite ingenious, don't you think?"

(22) The brother continues to explain about the portal and says, "A study of Sant'Antimo was made by the art historian Raspi-Serra, and completed in the 1960's. It brought us to conclude that the portal on the left side of the church of Santa Maria in San Quirico d'Orcia (approximately 20 km from Saint'Antimo), is none other than one of the two portals intended for the abbey. Perhaps the monastery, at that time, already in a state of decline, decided to give over the second portal to this other church."

20

23) **N**ow we are standing on the threshold of the portal. It is pleasing to see that this abbey always leaves its doors open. An unusual awareness begins to form in my mind. I have always considered churches, abbeys and monasteries as being splendid museums. In all of them I have always admired the architecture, paintings, and statues, while remaining absolutely indifferent to what is … invisible. At Sant'Antimo it is not the same. It's not only the beauty of the scenery, the overwhelming splendour of the abbey, a feeling of calm and peace that envelops you, on your arrival, but also the warm and invisible welcome that impresses you, as you enter the church. It's a soothing breeze that appeases every anxiety. It is an entering onto the road of a personal search.

Homo viator

24 Brother Giovanni interrupts my thoughts as he summons to me from within: "Francesco, come here! Just try to imagine how many people, believers and unbelievers, across the centuries, have walked on these very stones where we are now walking. How many pilgrims, how many wayfarers, now as then, have crossed the threshold of this abbey in search of the fount of salvation; how many astonished eyes, opened up to faith. But now look attentively! You too shall see what a person of the Middle Ages saw, on entering this church. Solid columns soaring up towards the sky like the trunks of magnificent trees, where the rays of the sun play about, to hide themselves between the capitals as if between the branches in a forest. It is the garden of Eden, the lost paradise. At the centre there is a mountain – the altar – on which the great tree of the cross is planted, the symbol of life and salvation. And then, if you look at the wooden ceiling, you can see the keel of a vessel. It is the ark of Noah, the vessel that moves across the flood waters, to carry those who believe to their heavenly homeland. These are symbols and messages expressed by the architecture in this church. A person from the Middle Ages,

cultured or uncultured, knew well how to read and decipher them. Today, the benches which occupy the central nave, impede a more global and enlarged vision, so to distract one's attention from the architectonic details with their artistic and symbolic value."

25 The brother remains silent, and seems to be lost in a far off vision. Then he sits on a bench, and continues, "Isolated in an exceptional way, and protected by the valley of the Starcia, today this abbey is situated at a certain distance from the major travel routes. In order to arrive at Sant'Antimo, you must deviate from the main road, but only if you know that this artistic monument exists, and you want to visit it. But this was not always so. During the 8th century, the Benedictines did not build their monasteries in distant zones, but on the more important crossroads of the epoch. During that period, characterised by continual factions, the abbeys stood as vital art-centres, particularly distinguished by their architecture. They were quiet, safe, and relatively tranquil havens, enjoying prosperous economical conditions. In order to give you a more exact idea, I have 'redrawn' the roads passing near

Sant'Antimo during the Middle Ages. Look here!"

26 I throw a look at the little map, and then gaze around. I watch the people as they enter. Some walk along looking upwards or turning their heads to right and left. Others, studying the guidebook, stop in front of each piece of art. Others are taking photos, while others kneel down on the kneeling stools, for a moment of meditation.

I draw close to brother Giovanni, and say, "What a lot of people come to see Sant'Antimo! They enter, they look, they walk about, and then go off. Who knows how much of all this will remain in their hearts?

Smilingly, the brother ruffles my hair with one hand. "Many men and women, during the past centuries, prayed, hoped, and believed under these vaults. They too entered, looked about, walked within, and then went off. But for them it was a journey of faith. The pilgrim that arrived from the north on the Via Francigena, or from the Maremma region on the west, stopped here in order to venerate the relics of Sant'Antimo, and in order to rest. Once having crossed the threshold of the church, the pilgrim entered onto

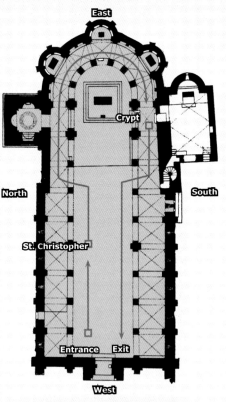

a severely outlined itinerary. Let us too walk along it. It was a symbolic, spiritual journey that had already commenced before entering the church. The column-bearing lions on both sides of the main portal represented the forces of evil, inducing the wayfarer to hasten his steps towards the inner side of the church, where to find refuge and salvation. So entering, he first made his way to the image of Saint Christopher, to venerate the patron saint of wayfarers. He then proceeded along the northern aisle, to follow, from the left, the entire ambulatory, until reaching the crypt, where he stopped to pray at the tomb of Sant'Antimo. On leaving the crypt, he moved towards the exit along the southern aisle, passing under the capital where Daniel is depicted in the lion's den.

"This walk represented the itinerary of the soul, which the believer had t o follow in order to pass from sin to grace, from death to life. An itinerary that began at the north, i.e. from cold, darkness, and death, to pass through the cross, symbol of Grace that saves and renews, and concluded at the south, in the sun, in the light, in life.

"In those days, many monks never left the monastery, making this symbolic journey within the walls of the church, as the only pilgrimage permitted throughout their life.

"This rite is relived today at Sant'Antimo during the week of Easter. To recall the original itinerary, a very touching and impressive procession accompanied by the Gregorian chant starts off from the main altar, crosses the entire length of the church, to enter the side aisles, and from the ambulatory, then returns again to end in front of the cross.

"And now, could we say a prayer together?"

SAINT CHRISTOPHER

The fame of Saint Christopher spread throughout Europe on account of the "Legenda Aurea" written by Jacopo da Varagine (13th century). According to this text, Christopher was a giant-sized youngster who had decided to put himself at the service of the most powerful man there could be. For this reason, firstly he served a king, then an emperor, and then the devil from which he learnt that Christ was the most powerful of all. This fact brought him to his conversion.

A saintly hermit taught him the precepts of charity. Intending to exercise himself in this virtue – as a preparation for baptism - he chose to live near a river where he could dedicate himself to the travellers wanting to cross over it. One night he was woken up by a beautiful child who begged him to take him across the river. The saint placed him onto his shoulders, but as he moved across the water, the weight of the boy always increased, so that only with great difficulty and by the use of a big long staff, he managed to arrive on the opposite bank. Here the child revealed himself to be Christ and prophesised his martyrdom as being briefly due. After his baptism, Christopher went to Lycia to preach – and to receive the crown of martyrdom.

The pilgrims had a very particular veneration for Saint Christopher, and precisely for this reason, institutions and congregations aimed at helping those travellers who had to overcome various types of difficulties relative to nature, were founded in his honour.

THE PILGRIMAGE ROUTE

The monastery of Sant'Antimo is not exactly on the Via Francigena. But this old idiomatic expression which declares that 'A more privileged abbey of the Roman Church and the Holy Empire does not exist in the whole of Italy'... gives us an idea of how much esteem and importance Sant'Antimo enjoyed during the Middle Ages. It therefore goes without saying that the pilgrims made a detour in order to stop at the abbey during their arduous and tiring journey.

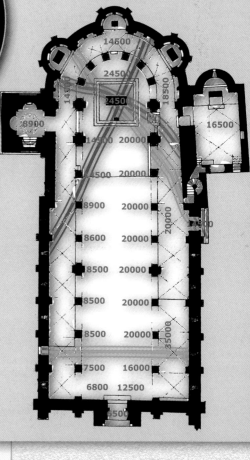

TELLURIC ENERGY

As was the custom in ancient times, so too during the Middle Ages – never were temples, castles or churches built without verifying their position in relation to the surroundings, the sun and the entire cosmos. Man tried to 'tap' the forces of the cosmos, in order to convey a special type of energy to a certain place. This energy is named telluric, and is multiplied by the presence of water, which intensifies the vibrations. The sage builders of cathedrals like that of Chartres or Santiago de Compostela, possessed an exceptional knowledge of energetic force influences and expressed it in architectonic ratios and measures.

At Sant'Antimo the altar is built where three underground streams – found at a depth varying from ten to twenty meters - cross over each other. This position causes an increase of energy along a precisely defined course. We begin with a Bovis unit of 6500 at the little door on the left, while around the altar we arrive up to a Bovis unit of 24000, to touch a maximum under the capital of Daniel in the lion's den, with a Bovis unit of 35000. Exactly the road followed by the pilgrims - the road to salvation.

Mr. Bovis, a French researcher of the 19th century, and the inventor of the "Bovis Scale" sensed this mutual relationship: "for every living organism there exists a vibration level of equilibrium, which corresponds to the state of health - 6500 Bovis unit. When one enters into contact with an incoherent energetic field that contains a lower level than ours, we lose energy; on the contrary, when we come into contact with an energetic field containing a higher vibration level more coherent than ours, we receive energy, and our vibration level is raised."

(27) So as not to disturb the silence in the church, brother Giovanni takes me to the cloister where we sit down on a low wall. He then says, "Francesco, I want to continue to tell you the story of Sant'Antimo. We have seen that the primitive nucleus was most probably a little oratory, after which the first monastery was then constructed. I had also explained how the founding of the monastery had been attributed to Charlemagne, forcing us to think about a frequent custom of that period by which the historic origins of a monument were falsified, or invented ex novo, in order to gain major importance for it.

"The vital Carolingian impetus permits the Benedictine community to enter its period of splendour. In fact, the abbot of Sant'Antimo held the title of Palatine Count (count and counsellor of the Holy Roman Empire), a public position of great importance conferred on him by the emperor. On studying the imperial parchments, the most important of which is undoubtedly that of Henry III (1051), and the Papal parchments preserved in various archives, a map can be traced of all the territories and churches which belonged to, or were under the jurisdiction of the abbey of Sant'Antimo. Within the areas stretching from Grosseto to Pistoia, and between Siena and Florence, 96 were properties between castles, lands, farms and mills, and 85 the complex number of monasteries, churches, parish-churches and hospitals. The major property of the community, over and above Sant'Antimo, was the castle of Montalcino. Here the Prior (the abbot's deputy), stayed in a residence, now incorporated in the fortress wall. Thus, at the beginning of the 12th century, the abbey was actually in a very satisfactory material and spiritual condition – well strengthened by the support of the Papacy, as by that of the Empire."

(28) We hear the sound of a door being opened. A brother comes forth, with a book in his hand. He sees us and slowly makes his way towards us. He is young, tall, and courteous. In a friendly way he says, "This marvellous sunlight invites me to come outside. At last I have a bit of time for studying today. I want to deepen my knowledge on a subject treated by Saint Augustine in one of his discourses. The open-air helps me to concentrate better. In this silence, surrounded by the beauty of nature, I appreciate more fully the gifts of the spirit."

(29) My guide greets him, and continues again to narrate: "But it was the year 1118 that signed the beginning of the apogee of Sant'Antimo. The count Bernard, son of Bernard, of the family Ardengheschi, ceded his entire patrimony of movables and real assets in his possession 'in the whole kingdom of Italy and in the whole region of Tuscany,' to Ildebrando, son of Rustico,

The Apogee

so that he could leave it to the abbey. One perceives the enormous entity of the donation, if one considers the very great sum of 1000 pounds paid by the monastery to Fortisguerra, brother of Bernardo. This sum was paid to obtain his consent, and the promise not to disturb the monks any longer in the enjoyment of their rights to the property.

"Such an enormous donation, even for the abbey of Sant'Antimo, was certainly an exception. This historic fact has been engraved on the steps of the main altar, in the form of a 'stone charter' as a perpetual memorial.

"The donation made in 1118 provided the necessary impulse for the construction of the new church. In fact, the abbot Guidone (1108 –1128), who received this donation, wanted Sant'Antimo to live up to its reputation as an imperial abbey. The new church, about to be built, had to be the most innovative and the most beautiful in artistic achievement. The reciprocal contacts between the Benedictine abbeys throughout Europe, was a particular characteristic of this period. The most important point of reference was the great Benedictine abbey of Cluny (Burgundy, France).

"Guidone, well aware of the famous reputation of the French architects, solicited plans from them for the new church, which seems thus to have its inspiration from the Benedictine abbey of Vignory, at Haute-Marne in Champagne (France), which dates to the year 1050."

(30) "Excuse me if I interrupt you, but I see that the transept is missing. At school I had learnt that many Romanesque churches were planned in the form of a cross. Here it seems

that the nave is narrow, where it should instead, be wider. Can you explain why this is so?"

Brother Giovanni looks at me with a satisfied expression. "You have made a very keen observation. I will now reveal you a little mystery. I would have preferred not to enter into the question as such, because there are no historic data in relation to this. Since you have made this question, however, I shall try to give you a full reply based on a quite reliable hypothesis. It is quite probable that between the first monastery (Sant'Antimo II), and the big abbey (Sant'Antimo IV), an intermediate church had been constructed (Sant'Antimo III). To sustain this hypothesis, they lay down the subsequent factors.

"Within the actual church, sculptures of a very high artistic value are found: the north portal and the south portal, the side posts of the sacristy door, some capitals situated in the north gallery, and

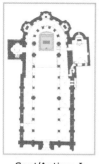

Sant'Antimo I

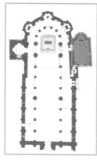

Sant'Antimo II

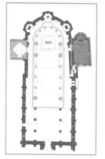

Sant'Antimo III

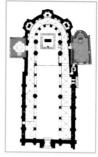

Sant'Antimo IV

other erratic capitals and fragments of decorative elements or little pillars. All these must have belonged to a building structure dating back to an epoch prior to the 12th century. This leads us to believe that during the 9th – 10th century, the abbey must have reached a great and magnificent splendour. But how could the Carolingian chapel, with a dimension of only 30 sq. meters, have space for 40 monks, as prescribed by Charles the Bald in the year 887?

"Historic data confirm that a Carolingian monastery did exist (Sant'Antimo II). Most probably, the primitive oratory (Sant'Antimo I), with the crypt that contains the sepulchre of the saint, is to be identified next to the Carolingian chapel. It is assumable that around the year 1000, the Benedictine monks had built a larger church on this crypt (Sant'Antimo III), of which only the bell tower still exists. Most probably it had been built in a detached position from the nave, according to an Italian architectonic tradition of that period.

"During the construction of the larger church, (12th century – Sant'Antimo IV), measures had to be taken in relation to the already existing structural bonding, adapting and cutting away the space of the presbytery, in order to insert it between the bell tower and the Carolingian chapel. And this is the likely reason why the choir zone of Sant'Antimo is narrower than the rest of the church. Has my explanation convinced you?

(31) "But now, let us return to the architecture of this abbey. The element which, more than any other,

confers
a   French
stamp to this church,
is the presence of the ambu-
latory and the radiating chapels. It is an innovative
plan, unique in Tuscany, and to be found in very few
churches in Italy: Santa Trinita in Venosa, the cathedral of Acerenza (Basilicata), the cathedral of Aver-
sa (Campania) and Santa Maria a Piè of Chienti
(Marche). The use of the ambulatory was not new in
Romanesque architecture. As early as the 6th and 7th
centuries, some churches were provided with passage-
ways behind the choir. One has to wait until the middle of the 11th century, however, before it expands. As
such, its use was not universal, because those territories depending on the Empire seem to have ignored
this architectural novelty. It is above all, along the pilgrimage routes of the epoch, that one finds churches with an ambulatory, as for example: Santiago de
Compostela, Saint-Gilles, Rome and Jerusalem. The
ambulatory, in fact, was born by the need of pilgrims
to walk round the martyrium, (place where the relics of the saint lie), and to stop there to pray. Do you
remember? We have already spoken about this fact!
Sant'Antimo is provided with an ambulatory because
it was situated at only a few kilometres from the Via
Francigena where the pilgrims passed en route to the
tomb of Saint Peter at Rome.

(32) "Other architectonic elements which connect the
church of Sant'Antimo to the artistic culture of France,
are the groin vaults of the ambulatory, and the side
aisles, as well as the height of the nave which soars up
to about 20 metres. One can also notice how the nave
has a layout of three distinct architectonic planes to order its height. On the ground plane, the large arches,
on the middle plane the triforium, or tribune (named
also 'matroneum'), and finally the plane of the windows, or cleresory, on the uppermost plane. This sub-
28 division into three planes does not exist in the Italian

Roman-
esque architec-
ture of the same period. Nonetheless, the basic model of the church
is substantially Lombard, as is the
wooden framework which covers
the nave, and the rhythmical line of
the arcade, interrupted by pillars.
"It is most probable that the nave
was subdivided along its length by

two transverse arches leaning on the cruciform pillars, while the apse closed up in a semi-spherical vault. To divide the roof into three parts, was a usage connected to two basic factors: For a purely aesthetic reason, by which more emphasis was given to the altar, and for a merely practical reason, by which to stop the spreading of the flames in case of fire. It is probable that a collapse destroyed these architectonic structures.

(33) "Towards the middle of the 12th century, the church was almost finished, but the façade remained incomplete. The abbey appeared to be solid and prosperous - at least this was the impression that it gave. But dark clouds were gathering over the territory of the monastery. Montalcino, at that time under the jurisdiction of the abbot of Sant'Antimo, proved to be of particular interest to Siena, as to Florence. In fact, since Siena could

Seal of the Vicar of the Abbot of Sant'Antimo, prior of the rectory of Sant'Egidio at Montalcino. (Florence - Bargello National Museum)

not expand to the north, on account of Florence, her rival, she tried to expand to the south. As early as July 1145, the Republic of Siena forced the abbot of San Salvatore to cede the castle of Radicofani along the Via Francigena. Just as if to support the political policy of Siena, Pope Clement III placed the parish of Montalcino under the Bishop of Siena, in a brief of 1189. Eleven years later, Philip Malvolti, podestà of Siena, and in command of its troops, attacked Montalcino. The town was assaulted, and the walls were destroyed. On 12th June 1212, after various events, an agreement was stipulated between the authorities of Montalcino, and the abbot of Sant'Antimo. With the authorities of Siena on one side, and those of Montalcino on the other, they confirmed that the abbey of Sant'Antimo must cede a quarter of the territory of Montalcino to the commune of Siena. The loss of Montalcino represented a heavy and irreparable blow for the abbot. It meant losing the most important centre of his jurisdiction. It was the beginning of the end. Siena would never abandon Montalcino again, and would begin to undermine the property of the monastery to such an extent, that in 1293 the abbey possessed only one fifth of all the properties found between Montalcino and Seggiano."

THE VIRGIN OF THE BELL TOWER

It could well be that this sculpture in alabaster was executed by a local artist. It cannot be placed on the same artistic level as that of the capitals found in the church, but does not lack a particular fineness. It seems to have been part of a pergula i.e. an internal architectonic division in the church (Sant'Antimo III cf. no. 30). It was put into the bell tower at an unknown date. It represents the Virgin with the four Evangelists. To recall somewhat its original position, the ambo has been embellished with a cast of it.

29

In this church, light, sound and stone exist together, to create an enchanting simbiosis. Each element permeates, moulds and lives in the essence of the other. The church is empty, but not silent. The walls throw back, without respite, the chant heard and absorbed by them, continually, for centuries. Its stones hold a world of melody and prayer which at every moment can free itself, to float through space and time, to touch, unperceived, the mind and the heart. This percipience is so tangible, that the music stave of a Gregorian melody still marks the wall of the ambulatory! Sant'Antimo may be an empty church, but ever remains a living church.

The Ambulatory

35 Brother Giovanni stands at the centre of the nave, and says, "The light flowing down from the large twin lancet window, guides the eye towards the main altar, centre of every church. Surrounded by seven arches, the altar stands at the middle of the choir. It has the form of a sarcophagus, according to an ancient tradition. The altar is reached by three steps, upon which the 'stone charter' which recalls the donation of Count Bernard is engraved, and which continues on the pier to the left of the altar. The choir is illuminated indirectly by the light from the radiating chapels, as frequently found in the Romanesque epoch. The choir floor dates to the 15th century. It is decorated with a number of half-moons, which form the coat of arms of the Piccolomini family."

nd the Presbytery

36 Now the brother moves to the right of the altar, to stop in front of a little railing at the head of a steep staircase made of high irregular steps, and says, "Here under the main altar, lies a little crypt, ventilated by a tiny window. It is the spot where the relics of the saints were placed. Strange to say, even if this crypt is placed under the main altar of the upper church, it is not in conformity to the 'canons' of 12th century architecture. Moreover, it has an anomalous position with reference to the general plan of the building. Are we thus in the readapted, primitive oratory, where the tomb of the holy martyr Antimo had stood for centuries? Where are his relics now? Stolen? Lost? Or still hidden here? The monks of the 12th century deliberately built the altar of the upper church exactly on the place where the body of the saint was laid. The throbbing heart of the abbey is thus under the altar. About 17 centuries of history are condensed here in this place. Here begins the very essence of the life of the abbey of Sant'Antimo, to remain miraculously intact up to the present day. The console of the little altar is a marble tombstone slab, dating back to the first centuries of the Church. It pertains to a young Christian, and bears an inscription in memory of the Consuls Rufinus and Eusebius (347 ac.). The 16th century fresco (author unknown) depicts the Deposition of Christ, King of martyrs, into the tomb."

37 "Do pardon my ignorance, but could you please explain to me who Saint Antimo was?"

"It is well to know," the brother explains, "that this name is borne by more than one saint, but only two of them can compete in claiming the title of patron saint of this abbey. With reference to the first one, the *"Acta Sancti Anthimi"* relates the story – perhaps embellished by legend – of a priest named Antimo, imprisoned at

the time of the Emperors Diocletion and Maximianus (304 –305). He healed, and so converted to the Christian faith Pinianus, the husband of Lycinia, niece of the Emperor Gallienus. From that moment, Pinianus did all that was possible, to protect Christians from persecution. Hidden in the villa of his protector, on via Salaria, Antimo also converted a pagan priest of the god Silvanus, and all his family. Accused of having destroyed the simulacrum of that divinity, Antimo is thrown into the Tiber with a stone around his neck, to emerge unharmed. Decapitated by order of the Consul Priscus, he was buried in the oratory where he habitually prayed. A Bolland historian of the 17th century surmises that in 781 Pope Hadrian I probably gave the relics of Saint Sebastian and Saint Antimo to Charlemagne, who then donated them to the abbey on the act of foundation. That the emperor had really brought these relics from Rome to the Starcia valley, is a fact yet to be verified. In medieval Tuscany, it was common usage to attribute the donation of relics of saints to Charlemagne. Saint Antimo of via Salaria was an authentic martyr of 304. Since 1658 his relics are venerated at Naples in the church of Sant'Antimo. The people of Castelnuovo dell'Abate celebrate his feast on 11th May.

(38) "The discovery of the cult of a Saint Antimo, which is not the homonymous saint of via Salaria, is quite recent. He was a deacon of Arezzo, who suffered martyrdom in 352 (or 304), together with the second Bishop of the city, Saint Donato. In fact, on examining the Aretine litanies, Saint Antimo appears in an ancient list of Aretine martyrs, and companions of Saint Donato. The first text found with reference to a Saint Antimo, which is not the Sabine one, is that of the *"Passio Donati"*. There are various editions, the oldest of which dates back to the first half of the 6th century. In this text, the story of the miracle of Saint Donato is narrated. The Bishop was celebrating Mass with his two deacons – Antimo and Asterio – during an ordination rite. Some pagans entered the church while Antimo was giving the communion from a glass chalice, and with violence they threw it on the ground, shattering it to pieces. After having put together all the pieces, Saint Donato found that one piece was still missing at the bottom of the chalice, but unconcerned about the matter, continued to serve the wine, without even a drop falling out of the chalice.

"This fact so astonished the pagans, that it caused their conversion. A month later, Saint Donato was arrested and put to death with other Christians, while

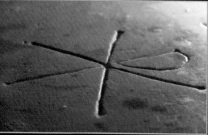

liturgical books, holy vessels and vestments were destroyed, as often came about during the persecution of Julian the Apostate. The companions who received the crown of martyrdom together with Saint Donato, were all buried at Pionta, a hill of Arezzo, while Saint Antimo was buried elsewhere. But where? Why not retain that Saint Antimo, in order to flee from the persecution, tried to find refuge in our Starcia valley (which during the 4th century was part of the Diocese of Arezzo) there to receive martyrdom and then be buried? Saint Donato and companions have their feast-day on 7th August.

"As time went by, and changes were brought about in this diocese (first of Chiusi, and then of Siena), Saint Antimo, deacon of Arezzo, became lost to memory, so permitting the Saint Antimo of via Salaria, to replace him as the abbey's patron saint.

"But my dear Francesco, I'm certain that in heaven these two martyrs of Christ are now united together in joy and happiness, for having shared in praising God by testifying so great a love for him."

On leaving the crypt, the visitor comes across the re-used door of the sacristy, opened in the 15th century during the period of the Bishops. The side posts and architrave bear sculptured decorations – 'girali'- on which avian figures are placed. The architrave is unfinished.

The brother stands still for a moment, and then continues again: "In the construction of this church, alabaster (called onyx in these zones), and travertine (from the local quarry of Castelnuovo dell'Abate), were utilised. These precious building materials were employed in executing the more noble elements, such as columns and capitals, while the walls were constructed with blocks of 'spongy' stone dug out from a quarry found along the road to Sant'Angelo in Colle. One of the characteristics of the alabaster is its translucence. At Sant'Antimo, therefore, the light penetrates, and passes through the stone to enliven its natural splendour.

"In the ambulatory this aspect is evidenced at a maximum when the sunbeams play across the stones in the morning. This is the most beautiful part of the church, the richest in decorative elements, where the best quality of stone was used. It is here, in this part that surrounds the altar – the heart of the Eucharistic celebration – that the builders began their work, to express the best of their art, and finish off each item with extreme attention. Each arch is embellished by its capital and column. Worth noting as well, is the small altar of the radiating chapel, continually watched over by the four eagles on the capital directly behind it. To the right of this chapel, the frescoes of two saints adorn the two blind arches. One saint is a pontiff (perhaps Saint Gregory the Great), the other a martyr saint (Saint Sebastian). The frescoes are attributed to Spinello Aretino (15th century), or else to a painter associated with Taddeo di Bartolo (14th-15th centuries)."

A MUSIC STAVE INSCRIBED ON THE WALL

A recent discovery has brought to light a stave of Gregorian music inscribed on the wall to the left of the sacristy door. It proves to be the remnant of a fresco. The pigmentation of the sinopite has passed through the plaster, so to stain the wall. A piece of Gregorian music, three meters long, and one meter high, is thus visible to us. Besides the notes, also the letters MINO are well distinguished, almost certainly the last four letters pertaining to the word DOMINO, written below the stave. An undulating file of notes precedes the letters to indicate the *jubilus* – a group of notes chanted on the same syllable (O). The opening-up of the sacristy door in the 15th century has cancelled the first part of the music stave. What melody does it now conceal?

Live therefore united together and with one accord, and reciprocally honour in one another that God, of which you are His living temple. (Rule)

The stone turns into a statue, music and poetry; and all flows up towards the stars across walls and glass-windows. Writing is architecture. (L. Plamondon)

also be presumed that the work had been accomplished by a single group of workers who had stayed at Auvergne.

(41) "Now fix your gaze on the majestic figure of Christ above the altar. It is of polychrome wood and dates back to the 13th century, reflecting a French influence (more exactly from Burgundy). It may well be that the execution of this work had been assigned to a sculptor – monk or layman – who stopped here for as much time as was necessary to realise this masterpiece. We know that the same sculptor executed the crucifix of Abbadia San Salvatore on Monte Amiata, prior to that of Sant'Antimo. Do you see - the Christ is standing upright on the cross, the head slightly bent towards the right, the eyes open (once coloured), with the arms almost horizontal, in order to embrace the world, and you also. The

(40) Brother Giovanni continues to speak: "The sculptures at Sant'Antimo denote a particularly high level of artistic quality, not only in relation to Sienese architecture, but also to that of the rest of Tuscany. And this notwithstanding the fact that they contain motifs habitually found in the Roman world (foliage – Mediterranean influence; geometric forms - Irish influence; biblical or mythological animals - Byzantine influence). This confirms the extraordinary talent of the masters who worked for this imposing enterprise. The refined geometric and vegetal motifs, so precise in design

knees are a little bent. The feet appear to be slightly detached from the altar, because after having formed a total union with the altar during the Eucharist, now the Body begins to ascend to heaven, to attain to that glory assigned him from all eternity. He suffers no more. He has risen and lives forever. In this instant the artist has fixed him."

and with intaglios so clear cut, denote a matrix which is to be found at Auvergne (Languedoc). The other capitals in the ambulatory, however, denote Lombard characteristics. It is therefore possible that two workshops, one French, and the other Lombard (Pavia) worked at Sant'Antimo. It may

Capitals and Sculptures

In silence he contemplates the face of the Christ. Then goes on to say, "Now I want to show you another artistic jewel, a masterpiece of medieval sculpture - the capital of Daniel in the lion's den, a work of the master of Cabestany, a real genius."

We move towards the second column from the main portal, placed along the southern side. Not to be struck by the inventive style, the artistic quality, and scenic impact of the capital at the top of this column, is impossible. As I admire the sculpture, my guide explains, "Travertine was used for the capital, and alabaster for the abacus, and it is surmounted on a pillar of a more recent period. On one side, we see Daniel in the attitude of prayer amongst the hungry lions; on the other side, the lions devouring his accusers..."

At this point, the brother takes out a little Bible from his pocket, and reads as follows: 'The accusers threw Daniel

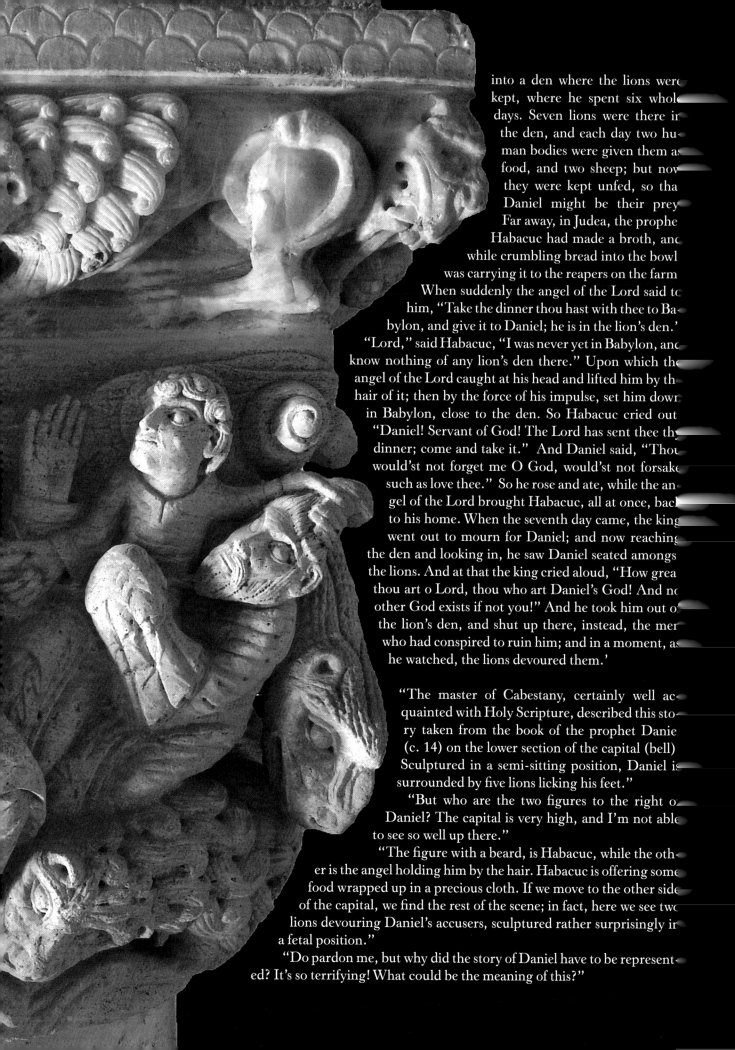

into a den where the lions were kept, where he spent six whole days. Seven lions were there in the den, and each day two human bodies were given them as food, and two sheep; but now they were kept unfed, so that Daniel might be their prey. Far away, in Judea, the prophet Habacuc had made a broth, and while crumbling bread into the bowl was carrying it to the reapers on the farm. When suddenly the angel of the Lord said to him, "Take the dinner thou hast with thee to Babylon, and give it to Daniel; he is in the lion's den.' "Lord," said Habacuc, "I was never yet in Babylon, and know nothing of any lion's den there." Upon which the angel of the Lord caught at his head and lifted him by the hair of it; then by the force of his impulse, set him down in Babylon, close to the den. So Habacuc cried out "Daniel! Servant of God! The Lord has sent thee thy dinner; come and take it." And Daniel said, "Thou would'st not forget me O God, would'st not forsake such as love thee." So he rose and ate, while the angel of the Lord brought Habacuc, all at once, back to his home. When the seventh day came, the king went out to mourn for Daniel; and now reaching the den and looking in, he saw Daniel seated amongst the lions. And at that the king cried aloud, "How great thou art o Lord, thou who art Daniel's God! And no other God exists if not you!" And he took him out of the lion's den, and shut up there, instead, the men who had conspired to ruin him; and in a moment, as he watched, the lions devoured them.'

"The master of Cabestany, certainly well acquainted with Holy Scripture, described this story taken from the book of the prophet Daniel (c. 14) on the lower section of the capital (bell) Sculptured in a semi-sitting position, Daniel is surrounded by five lions licking his feet."

"But who are the two figures to the right of Daniel? The capital is very high, and I'm not able to see so well up there."

"The figure with a beard, is Habacuc, while the other is the angel holding him by the hair. Habacuc is offering some food wrapped up in a precious cloth. If we move to the other side of the capital, we find the rest of the scene; in fact, here we see two lions devouring Daniel's accusers, sculptured rather surprisingly in a fetal position."

"Do pardon me, but why did the story of Daniel have to be represented? It's so terrifying! What could be the meaning of this?"

"Francesco, as already explained, the Christian culture of the Middle Ages abounds in symbolism, which can also enrich spiritual life. Saint Augustine, in a comment on the psalm 132, draws a comparison between three types of men in the church, and three personages of the Old Testament – Noah represents the priests, Job the laymen, and Daniel the monks. To tell the story of Daniel means thus to instruct and admonish the monks at Sant'Antimo, and all the pilgrims in transit at the abbey. Saint Jerome offers another key of interpretation in a commentary on the story of Daniel, creating a parallelism between the figure of the Prophet and that of Christ. In the same way as Daniel, who had been accused unjustly, and thrown into the lion's den - symbol of hell with the devils – came out victorious on account of his faith in the living God, so too Christ, the Just One without sin, accused by his enemies, nailed to the cross, and laid in the tomb, rises on the third day, to overcome death forever. 'Praise to thee, Lord, thou hast taken me under thine protection, and baulked my enemies of their will; I cried out to the Lord my God (raised hand of Daniel) and thou did'st grant me recovery. So did'st thou bring me back, Lord, from the place of shadows, rescue me from the edge of the grave.' This versicle from the psalm 29, expresses the hailing cry of Christ, the Son, in thankfulness towards the Father, on the morning of the resurrection."

"I begin to understand."

(44) "The master of Cabestany also tried to apply an allegorical interpretation to the narrative. On the abacus (upper section of the capital), monsters, dragons and lions biting their tails and tearing each other to pieces are depicted. These horrible, ferocious beasts symbolise death and the devil defeated by the risen Christ. **40** The two birds biting the ser-

pent, assume a similar sense - life winning over death. On the opposite side of the abacus, fruit and flowers are being sapped by little treacherous coiling serpents, to signify that during the life of everyone who believes in the risen Christ, many mortal dangers lie insidiously hidden."

Brother Giovanni looks at the capital, and then at the twin lancet window above the presbytery. "Do you know what I saw last year during the spring period? During the month of April the sunrays pass through the twin lancet window and light up the capital for a few minutes. This leads us to think that in constructing this church they may well have left, as yet, another symbolic sign – the symbol of the resurrection lit up during that month when Easter is generally celebrated. This capital could deliberately have been collocated, therefore, in this position."

THE MAS

The name – Master of Cabestany - was invented in 1944, by the art historian Josep Gudiol. But who was the Master of Cabestany? Where did he come from? All this information remains hidden to us, but we can get to know him through his works of art (about twenty) spread between Catalonia, Languedoc, Roussillon and Tuscany. The master of Cabestany (a tiny town near Perpignan – France) was a wandering sculptor. Many of his works were realised for Benedictine monasteries. Most probably he travelled with his atelier, according to the custom of the epoch, in order to comply with the demands of the monks.

This sculptor is a 'key personage' to 12th century Mediterranean sculpture. He possesses a unique style, which betrays a strong character. How do we recognise the works of Cabestany? In the first

(45) "And this isn't all," my friend explains, "because also two other casts belonging to the master Cabestany exist. The first work consists of a base for the large paschal candle. The original is to be found in the Museum of Sacred Art at San Casciano Val di Pesa, near Florence. The artistic column came from the church of San Giovanni in Sugana, one of the many churches which were subject to the abbey of Sant'Antimo. One is led to believe that this work, originally executed for the abbey, had, for some unknown motive, landed up in this tiny country church. Sculptured in marble from the Montagnola quarry (near Siena), the column depicts the cycle of Christ's infancy (Annunciation, Nativity, news to shepherds, bath of child). On a trunk 70 cm high and with a diameter of 28 cm, ten figures, six animals, and a star have been sculptured! Do you realise what an exceptional technical ability this sculptor possessed? This is the unquestionable style of Cabestany!"

"But why sculpture nativity scenes on the base for a candle used at Easter?"

"A very interesting question, Francesco. The reason is as simple as it is profound. From time immemorial the baptismal rite is connected to Easter. Water is an essential item for Baptism; it purifies and regenerates. For medieval Christians, the water that had touched the pure and holy infant, Jesus, when immersed in the basin, represented the purifying of all water used for baptising. The symbology on the base used for the Paschal candle is strictly related to that of the Daniel capital. By virtue of the baptismal water, one is re-born to a new life, to continue along the way that leads to the resurrection. The pilgrimage made by us a little while ago is thus again evoked. Starting from the little north-side door at the Baptismal Fount, which signs a new life in Christ, the itinerary finishes on the opposite side, at he capital of Cabestany – to consign an extreme certainty - the resurrection of the flesh."

Brother Giovanni turns towards the (46) statue of the Virgin behind him, and continues, "On the 11th May, the patron feast-day, the people of Castelnuovo dell'Abate carry in procession a copy of the Virgin of Sant'Antimo. It's a wooden statue of the 13th century (Um-

R: HIS STYLE AND PERSONALITY

place, our master is a virtuoso in composing. He manages to place together many figures on tiny surfaces. No empty space is left in his sculptures. In portraying the figures, the master follows a precise norm, so as to be recognised by the faces, eyes and hands that give the sculpture a 'wild' and 'brutish' note. This liberal form of expression is accompanied by a marked attention towards details. It is sufficient to see how he treats the folds of the clothing. In short, the anonymous sculptor gets his inspiration from Roman antiquity; he knows well how to utilise the bas-relief technique, so as to create works that denote a typical Romanesque stamp.

He works on every type of stone: marble, alabaster, travertine, limestone; and sculptures on every kind of support: capitals, tympanum, modillions, friezes, candelabrum. He deals with a variety of iconographic themes: themes relating to the Old and New Testament (above all the Nativity cycle, and the Marian cycle), and hagiographic themes. Beasts, animals and angels are ever present throughout his works.

41

Beginning of the Paschal Vigil:
The *Exultet* sung in front of the Paschal Candle,
symbol of the risen Christ.

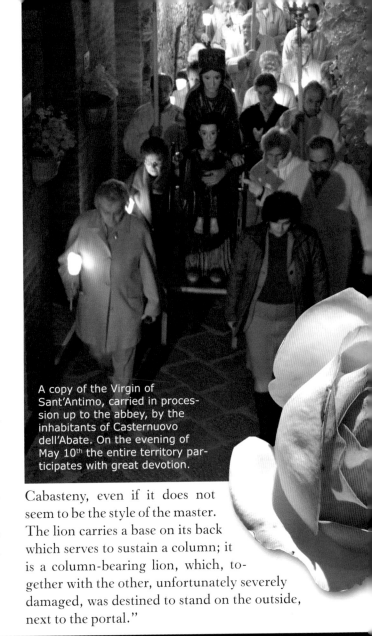

A copy of the Virgin of Sant'Antimo, carried in procession up to the abbey, by the inhabitants of Casternuovo dell'Abate. On the evening of May 10th the entire territory participates with great devotion.

brian school). The Virgin is sitting on a well- decorated throne, and holds the child Jesus on her knees. A portrayal of this type was frequent in the Middle Ages, when the Virgin was venerated as the 'seat of wisdom.' The date on which this statue arrived at Sant'Antimo, is unknown, but she is cited in 1655 as a 'powerful Protectress' of the inhabitants of the region. Still most venerated, the Virgin of Sant'Antimo protects the abbey and its children from many dangers, and grants them many favours. Two other works belonging to the abbey, are currently in the museum of Montalcino: a crucifix from the 11th or 12th century painted in distemper, and a Bible from the 12th-13th century."

Cabasteny, even if it does not seem to be the style of the master. The lion carries a base on its back which serves to sustain a column; it is a column-bearing lion, which, together with the other, unfortunately severely damaged, was destined to stand on the outside, next to the portal."

(47) Once again we move towards the exit. On the inner side of the façade I notice some vestiges of plaster. Before I could ask a question, the brother explains, "This plaster suggests that the walls of the church may well have been partially decorated with frescoes, following the custom of the epoch."

He then places his hand on a sculptured lion next to the portal, and continues: "These lions are in travertine, and one of them, as can be seen, is still perfectly preserved. Some art critics would ascribe it to

THE TABERNACLE

The tabernacle door presents another cast of the Master of Cabestany. It is a detail from the sarcophagus of Saint Saturninus at Saint Hilary (France). Under the blessing hand of the Father, the two angels incense the tomb of the saint. In these two figures, so dynamic and solemn at the same time, vigour and delicateness are united together according to the style of the sculptor.

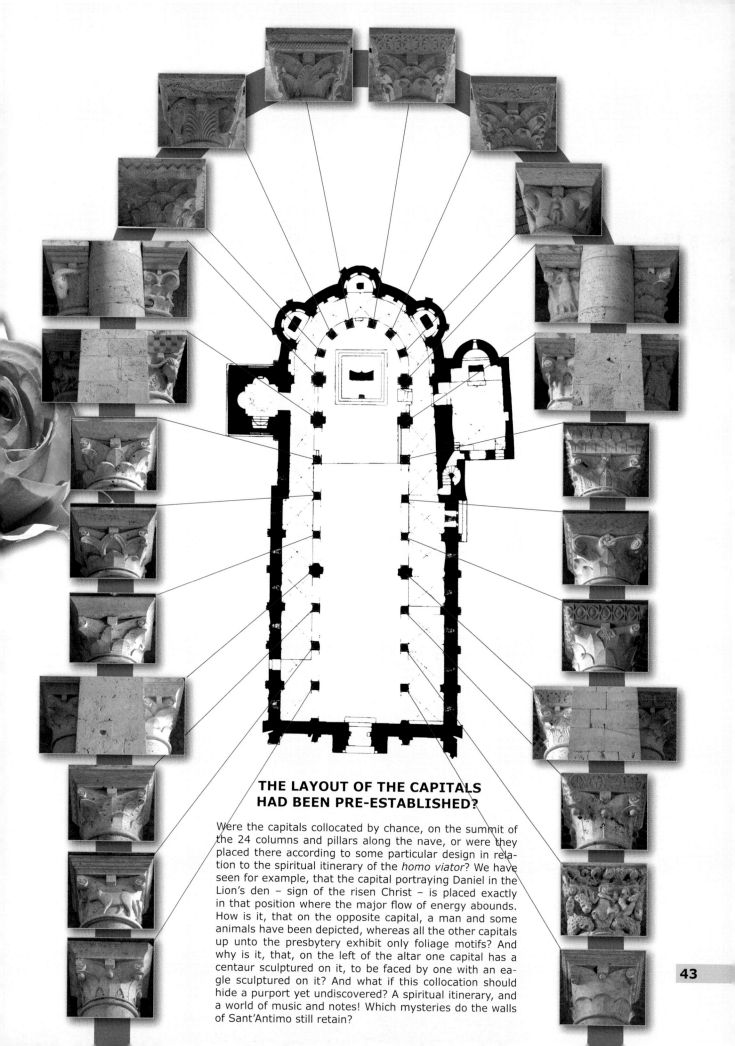

THE LAYOUT OF THE CAPITALS HAD BEEN PRE-ESTABLISHED?

Were the capitals collocated by chance, on the summit of the 24 columns and pillars along the nave, or were they placed there according to some particular design in relation to the spiritual itinerary of the *homo viator*? We have seen for example, that the capital portraying Daniel in the Lion's den – sign of the risen Christ – is placed exactly in that position where the major flow of energy abounds. How is it, that on the opposite capital, a man and some animals have been depicted, whereas all the other capitals up unto the presbytery exhibit only foliage motifs? And why is it, that, on the left of the altar one capital has a centaur sculptured on it, to be faced by one with an eagle sculptured on it? And what if this collocation should hide a purport yet undiscovered? A spiritual itinerary, and a world of music and notes! Which mysteries do the walls of Sant'Antimo still retain?

The Hour of Sext

Attend diligently to prayer at the established hours and times. In the oratory nothing must be done to contradict the purpose for which it was created and the name it bears, so that he who has time and wants to pray over and above the established hours, be not impeded by who deems it necessary to do other things there. When praying to God with psalms and hymns, meditate within the heart that which the lips pronounce. (Rule)

(48) I'm hardly aware of how the time is passing. From the southern portal a brother enters the church and walks silently along the ambulatory, to disappear into the bell tower. A few seconds later, the rhythmic sound of a ringing bell is heard. It is 12.40 p.m. Brother Giovanni says, "So as not to lose contact with the Absolute, every three hours the bell summons the community to praise God. Within five minutes, Sext will be sung, after which we go to lunch."

My personal guide remains silent. The brothers form a slow and solemn procession, and enter the presbytery to place themselves ac-cordingly, in the choir stalls. The plainchant, which is also a prayer, begins. A copy of the psalms sung in Latin, fortunately provided with an Italian translation, helps me to follow the singing more closely.

(49) I try to concentrate as best I can, but am frequently tempted to watch the brothers during the ritual gestures, which accompany the singing. The use of Latin is however, quite perplexing – a language familiar only to few. More convenient would be the use of Italian. The plainchant is also very beautiful, but difficult to fol-low. So I can neither sing nor pray with them, to remain excluded, and just an onlooker! Yet, next to me I notice how the people get up, as the brothers get up, while in the front row, some youngsters bow down lowly during the *gloria* (dossology). Some of the people keep the text closed – perhaps they are unable to understand Italian, but their features and their attitude reveal a deep attention, undoubtedly caused by the moving and mystic atmosphere created by the liturgy. I too want to comprehend. I too want to participate.

Lunch and Coffee with the Brothers

(50) The liturgy having thus ended, the brothers leave the church in silence. With a winning glance brother Giovanni asks me, "Would you like to come to lunch with us?"

Dash it! Magnificent! Just what I hoped for, but didn't dare to ask! My reply is more restrained than are my thoughts. "Well, if I won't disturb too much, it will really be a pleasure."

The brother continues his 'lesson' while we stroll towards the brothers' living quarters as he says, "The monks of the Middle Ages, just as nowadays, on leaving the church after Sext went to the refectory. According to the Benedictine tradition, the refectory was always built parallel to the church, to signify a parallelism between the earthly table where the monks dined, while listening to holy reading, and the heavenly table i.e. the Mass celebrated in the church. Holy Scripture in fact, says, 'Man does not live by bread alone, but from every word that comes forth from the mouth of God.' (Deut. 8, 3). Actually the refectory and adjacent rooms have been transformed into our living quarters, so losing their original functions."

Then, all at once, he changes the subject, and asks me, "By the way, did you manage to follow Sext? You seemed rather distracted."

Quite embarrassed, and somewhat irritated, I reply, "Well, to say the truth, I made an enormous effort, but I don't understand Latin, and much less why you make all those gestures during the prayer."

"It's quite normal," he replies, "one needs time to get acquainted with our liturgy; just as with a friend. It requires time to get to know him, and to get accustomed to him."

₅₁ Then, taking up the previous subject of conversation where it had been interrupted, he goes on to say, "You seemed quite pleased, but also somewhat aston-

ished by my invitation to come to lunch with us. The vocation to offer hospitality, one of the characteristics of the Premontratensien Regular Canons, exists from the times of our founder. Saint Norbert recalls three duties: towards God, by attention to the altar, towards the brother, in correcting him, and towards the guests, in offering hospitality."

At the door of the refectory, a brother awaits us.

"This is the Prior," brother Giovanni explains.

I feel a bit nervous.

The Prior puts out his hand to greet me, and with a big smile says, "Welcome! We are happy to have you at table with us. I hope it will prove to be a pleasant experience for you."

₅₂ He then takes me into the spacious refectory hall. I recall how broth-

Overcome the instincts of the flesh by fasting and abstinence from food and drink, in as much as health permits. If someone is incapable of fasting, he must however avoid eating between meals, except in case of illness.

From the beginning of the meal until the end, always listen to the accustomed reading without discussions or making noise, so that not only the mouth be fed, but also your ears be hungering for the word of God. (Rule)

er Giovanni had explained that up until 1966, this hall had been a stable. What an incredible change! It is one o'clock.

Before sitting down to lunch, the brothers stand bowed down, one in front of the other, as the prayer to bless the food is said. I notice that a liturgical accent is present also at lunch. No one speaks in the refectory. As the community eats in silence, a brother reads a passage in *recto tono*, from some edifying book, which can be either of a religious, historic, philosophic, or biographic nature, or contemporary literature. I recall the words of brother Giovanni - "not only the body must be nourished, but also the mind and the spirit". After having finished reading, the reader will take some nourishment as well. On fast-days the brothers eat less meat, and abstain from drinking wine. I was told that a woman cooks their meals during the week.

After lunch, each brother takes his plate to the kitchen to be washed. I follow along, and do the same. The only sound to be heard is that of the water, as the plates are placed on the draining rack. I feel rather awkward, but try to help all the same.

As soon as the 'silent' plate-₅₃ washing is finished, my guide whispers, "Francesco, come here, I want to acquaint you with my community. Once lunch is over, and the dishes are washed, this is the nicest moment, because some free time remains to enjoy each other's compa-

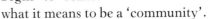

ny, while on Sundays and holidays, friends and visitors are also invited. An opportunity is offered to speak, to joke, to exchange daily experiences and opinions as we get to know one another a bit better. If the weather permits, we take a walk, while during the winter season we get together in the hall of Saint Catherine. You are very fortunate, because today, 6th June, is the feast-day of Saint Norbert."

We walk along the short corridor, which connects the refectory to the Saint Catherine hall. On entering, we go down a few steps. It is a bright and spacious hall with plain pieces of furniture. At the centre, there is a long wooden table. On the shelves, and other low furniture, theologic, and religious reviews lie about. On the walls photos and sculptures are displayed. It is the hall where each morning the Chapter is kept. Until some time ago, it had a less noble use; it was in fact, a cellar.

(54) In the hall, seven or eight brothers are all chatting away merrily. At first I just look on, without saying anything. I notice some friends of the community joking together in a very friendly manner with the fathers. The atmosphere is calm and relaxed. It puts me on my

ease, just like being at home. And then there is no TV to ruin the conversation. Little by little I begin to realise what it means to be a 'community'.

Almost immediately, I become aware of some brothers speaking with a foreign accent. I'm unable to place their nationality. I turn towards the religious beside me and say, " Excuse me, but are you not Italian?" From behind his glasses he fixes me with an ironic smile, and replies,

"Well, as such, you can take your choice. I am French, Senagalese, and Italian by adoption! And you, Francesco, where are you from?"

"Well… as such, only from Parma!"

The nice priest then continues in a more severe tone: "You see, quite a few nationalities are mixed together here; some of us are French, with Italian citizenship, one is English, or more precisely from Wales, and two are Italians. We are a European community, similar to the stylistic influences present in the church. The community and the church express the same European and international vocation. By the way, did you like the church?"

"Very much indeed," I reply enthusiastically.

With these witticisms we begin to get to know each other, and I feel ever more at home.

(55) The atmosphere takes on quite a gay tone. Cakes and coffee are brought in, and placed on the table. I want to get to know their daily timetable. Having arrived only after the daily Mass at 9.15 a.m., I'm interested to know what other religious practices are done before that hour.

"We get up at 5.15 a.m.," explains the brother, "to begin Matins at 5.45 a.m. This liturgical prayer

consists in reciting a number of psalms in *recto tono*, as a base to the daily liturgy. We read the Bible in Latin, and so too the Fathers of the Church. After this, during summer as in winter, a long moment of personal meditation follows, in the silence of the church. The personal dialogue with God, and attention to the Divine Word, enriches this moment in a very particular way. Lauds is sung at 7.00 a.m. It is a pity that you were not present at this prayer of praise made by the entire Church to its creator and its Saviour. The psalm 62, which begins with *Deus, deus meus es tu, ad te de luce vigilo* (O God, you are my God, at dawn I search for you), unites us to the whole of creation as the morning sun explodes across the earth. It is a hymn of joy, a song of glory, by which we, tiny particles of the cosmos, love God, praise and bless His Holy Name. On returning to visit us, you should try to remain somewhat longer so as to experience personally the stirring emotions and sublime considerations inspired during this magnificent liturgy."

The brother drinks his cup of coffee, and then adjoins, "Another moment when our prayer reaches more intensive heights of intimacy with the Saviour, is during the vigil held each week, on Saturday, roundabout midnight. During the deep silence of the night, while darkness muffles and shrouds every quiver of earthly life, the brothers sing psalms as they await the resurrection of Christ, renewed every Sunday during the celebration of the Holy Eucharist. This is no sacrifice for us, as you can well imagine, but rather, an act of love, full of joy – because - Francesco, as you know, love believes, hopes, keeps watch, and prays." At these words, all the voices around me fade away, while the words pronounced by the brother penetrate like a subtle arrow, to touch the innermost centre of my being. Never, until this moment, had I ever been aware that the words of faith are also words of love.

The bell... 'voice of the spouse'... is ringing once more. It is already 2.40 p.m.! How quickly the time has passed. None will begin after five minutes.

SAINT CATHERINE AND THE ABBEY

It is a custom to furnish the main halls of the monastery with a name. The great Sienese saint was well acquainted with the community of Sant'Antimo, reason enough for a hall being dedicated to her. The saint had stayed at the abbey for a few weeks during the summer of 1377. Her presence and preaching drew a great number of people, who confessed themselves to the Dominican Friars who had accompanied the saint. She was a friend of the abbot of Sant'Antimo - fra Giovanni di Gano of Orvieto – who assisted her at her death at Rome in 1380.

After None, my brother-guide takes me to the sacristy, where an opening in the west wall gives access to a steep, narrow, spiral staircase dating to the 12th century. It leads up to the tribune. Once arrived at the top of the staircase, I lean over the parapet of the twin lancet window situated above the nave, in order to admire the spectacular aerial perspective of the church. The brother opens an old renaissance-style door. The architrave and side posts are made of 'serena' stone. On the inside there is a space where a little German organ is kept, with seven stops for liturgical use. It dates back to the sixties. Another door takes us into the Bishop's apartment, set in the south tribune. The first room was the dining hall. It is decorated with pastoral frescoes and provided with a fireplace. Two other simpler rooms follow. Quite de-

cisively, this abbey reveals rather a number of odd things. Brother Giovanni perceives my astonishment, and says, "You see, the big imperial abbey of the 12th century was transformed, along with time, into the temporary residence of the Bishops of Montalcino, and subsequently even into a farmhouse! Magnificence and decadence.

"Do you recall how the Republic of Siena had inflicted a mortal blow on the abbot of Sant'Antimo, when they besieged and occupied the castle of Montalcino? Well, in 1291, Pope Nicholas IV ordered the Benedictine community of the abbey to unite themselves to the Guglielmites, a reformed branch of the Benedictines, who lived in a narrow valley near Castiglione della Pescara. By this decision the Pope hoped to give renewed vigour to the religious community of Sant'Antimo, by then prey to hundreds of difficulties. It is a fact that the Guglielmites were known to be 'men filled with a fervour for piety, contemplation, and chastity'. Amidst the many negative events, we must also remember that the devastating pestilence of 1347 decimated a third of the European population, and the monasteries were not to be spared. Notwithstanding the efforts made by Saint Catherine to reform the community, it continued to slither and slide ever more in the dark. From 1397 until 1404, the abbey was 'administered, directed, and governed' by fra Bartholomeu di Simone, Bishop of Cortona. But the worst was yet to come... On the 4th August 1439, the abbot Paul of Castelnuovo dell'Abate was imprisoned for his villany. After him, the community was guided by two other abbots, the last being

the Guglielmite, Herculaneum. In 1462, in the chapel of Saint Benedict (Carolingian chapel) the last and ultimate Chapter of the Guglielmites was held, and the Benedictine community so breathed its last in this valley. 530 years will pass, before the liturgical chant shall be heard again at Sant'Antimo.

(58) "As a matter of fact, the great Pope of the Renaissance, Pius II (from the Piccolomini of Pienza), in 1462 suppressed the abbey and entrusted its goods to the Bishop Cinughi, first Ordinary of the new Diocese of Montalcino – Pienza, created on 13th August of the same year. The Supreme Pontiff cited this event in his commentaries, as follows: 'Through the negligence of its last abbots, it (the abbey) has come to such a degree of poverty that it no longer possess any tem-

stones had been utilised for the construction of the neighbouring houses, and it is sufficient to dig in the field facing the main portal, to discover remnants of the monastery, pieces from capitals etc. In order to avoid the worst, it seems evident that the new proprietors of the abbey intervened only in order to adjust the still existing parts. The first Bishops, in fact, restored the roof, and perhaps heightened also the tribune walls, thus modifying them. They modified the presbytery by opening a door in the wall, which, from the Carolingian chapel gives direct access to the church. It is not so easy to identify the exact points where they had intervened. It was the third bishop, Agostino Patrizi, that created the apartment that we are now visiting."

"It is really quite fascinating, but was it not rather an awkward place for a renaissance prelate?"

"Yes - but the bishops did not stay here all the year round, preferring to remain at their residence at Montalcino, or at Castelnuovo dell'Abate. They visited the abbey mainly to receive the taxes. The historian Canali related an amusing anecdote in respect to this. He

poral property. The abbot who ruled over the monastery in these times, an extravagant man, and lacking concern, has neglected or sold that material property which remained, and squandered all to such an extent, that the bread of sorrow and the water of misery was all that could sustain it.' But this Pope was exaggerating, because the abbey was still quite prosperous. He simply wanted to change his town of birth Corsignano, into a Renaissance city, called Pienza, in order to give it also a Bishop (none other than his nephew), with territories and ruling power. Sant'Antimo was a very interesting pawn for the realisation of his project."

(59) "But why build an apartment in the tribune? Would it not have been easier to adapt the already existing rooms around the cloister?"

"The very fact that they built above the chapter hall and then in the tribune, signifies that in the 15th century various parts of the main structure had already collapsed - such as the cloister, some sections of the chapter hall, the library, the dormitory, and

the store-houses... The

wrote: 'On the 11th May, men from Castel del Piano brought into the church of Saint'Antimo, as payment for taxes, 16 pounds and many dishes, i.e. 100 pieces of crockery for the use of the monastery, and above all, for the bishop of Montalcino, *inter Missarum Solemnia.* They carried the said pottery in two sacks. When the receiver of the bishop or abbot said, "There are not one hundred pieces here," they responded: "If there are not, we will make them." And as they threw the sacks down on the ground, one could hear the breaking of the crockery.'

"A positive note, can however, be found amidst this progressive abandonment."

"Why do you say this?"

"For a very simple reason. The decline has contributed in leaving intact the Romanesque church. If the monks would have remained here, the abbey most likely would have undergone architectural remodelling, according to the later Renaissance or Baroque styles, as had happened to many medieval churches."

(60) The tribunes above the aisles are connected along the western side by a corridor, most probably adjoined during the period of the bishops. It runs along the inner side of the façade wall, and is upheld by four little semi-circular arches, while on the eastern side, they follow the curve of the apse, to form and sustain the upper ambulatory. The north tribune is not divided into rooms, thus permitting the twin lancet windows to pass more light on the nave. The archaeological finds discovered in the cloister and elsewhere, are here preserved.

We stop in front of a high, narrow (61) door, just where the wall of the north tribune is about to curve in order to form the apse. Brother Giovanni looks at his watch, and then at me. In rather an amused way, he asks me,

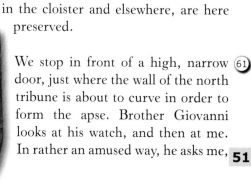

"Will your legs be able to carry you up to the top of the bell tower? Climbing up these stairs is quite exhausting, but the view that one encounters up there amply rewards every effort made. Come! Let's go up! I shall tell you more secrets about this abbey."

I begin to climb the stairs, while at every floor the view continues to change...the roof over the north aisle, the roof of the abbey, then ...the pigeons sheltering in the spaces in the walls, on the windowsills, or under the eaves... At last we arrive! From the terrace that covers the bell tower, the view is breathtaking – certainly on account of the many steps we climbed! From up here, the entire valley can be seen. The horizon stretches out, over and above the profile of the hills. As the wind tears lightly at his tunic, brother Giovanni points out some nearby places, and some others further away, hidden amongst the green hills. "This is 'our' property – lands, fields, fruit orchards! But just look at the strange aspect that everything assumes from on high! The roofs of the two apses look like wheels made from Chinese fans. And the cypress from up here no longer seems so tall and stately. There, on the southern side of the abbey are our living quarters. Lower down, and somewhat hidden by the walls surrounding the cloister, there are two reception halls for the guests – the 'San Norberto' hall, and the 'Sant'Agostino' hall. A little lower still, under the oak tree, the Scout centre and the small toilet block can be seen. On the opposite side of the road, in a hollow excavated in the hill, below Castelnuovo dell'Abate, we built a big centre (in the year 2000), where groups of visitors can stay. It is the Tabor Hostel. Later on, we shall make a visit there..."

From afar off, the church-clock of Castelnuovo dell'Abate strikes the hour. The brother continues to explain, "The bell tower of the abbey also has its bells. Here they are! Two of them! One bears the date MC-CXVIIII (1219), and the name of the abbot Ugo (1216 –1222). From this date onwards, the toiling of this bell has continued to measure the hours, to call to prayer, and to announce oncoming danger. It seems strange to you? Most probably, during the period that ran from the 14th to the 16th century, the abbey was a fortified and protected place, where the inhabitants of the surrounding countryside could find refuge in case of danger. The top of the roof, as also the top of the bell tower were crenelated, whilst a secret underground passage proceeding from the crypt in an eastern direction, was used in order to escape unnoticed. This tunnel which in part has collapsed, was definitely closed to visitors in 1970, for safety measures. Before going down from here, however, I would like to say something more about the community."

While he's speaking, I notice a stain on his white tunic, and point it out to him. He has a look at it, and with a smile he says, ""Being white, this is quite normal. Even if it is a becoming colour, it gets dirty quite easily. To keep the tunic clean as long as possible is a problem, because we can't change the tunic every day."

"But why choose a white tunic? Would it not have been better to choose a brownish one, as the Capuchins have, for example?"

"The white colour has been passed down to us from our founder, Saint Norbert. He wanted to unite the ministry of the priesthood to poverty, and for this reason chose the woollen clothing of the poor, who dressed like this in the 12th century. On account of constant washing, the colour slowly turned white. To the canons of that period, always dressed in black, he justified his choice by explaining that the signifi-cance was symbolic. He and his brothers had chosen the colour borne by the angels at the Resurrection of Christ, because they too were called to announce the risen Christ."

"You are therefore like the Dominicans?"

"The opposite rather, because Saint Dominic had copied much from the Premonstratensien Regular Canons."

"I must say that I remain quite disorientated amidst all these religious orders. I can't understand what difference exists between you, the friars, and the monks, except for the different colour of the tunic – when it is not dirty, of course."

"The explanation is very simple, Francesco. Look at that field of flowers down there."

I turn my gaze eastwards, to see a field spotted with red poppies and orange-coloured flowers. It resembles an impressionist painting of Monet.

"In His field, which is the Church, God has planted many types of flowers, all differing from one another, and it is exactly these contrasts that create its beauty."

Brother Giovanni gives another look at the flowering field, and goes on to say, "I shall try to illustrate briefly the specific characteristics of the Regular Canons. In one of his speeches, Saint

A Spiritual... Chat

Augustine speaks thus: 'The cleric therefore assumes two commitments – consecrated life, and clerical service. The consecration is connected to his inner life, while the clerical service, placed on his shoulders by the Lord, for the benefit of His people, is to be considered more a weight than an honour.' In the formulation of our perpetual religious profession, we say as follows: 'I, brother...., in offering my person, dedicate myself to the church of Sant'Antimo.....' (offerens, trado meipsum Ecclesiae Sancti Anthimi). These two quotations hold, and reveal the threefold fragrance that the white flower of our tunic emanates.

(64) "Each new religious order, just like every reform made in the Church, always draws its inspiration from the first Community of Christians at Jerusa-

In a similar way, no one must accomplish anything only for personal interest, but all that you do, be it done for the community – employing major efforts and zeal, than working for oneself. In fact, it is written that charity does not seek personal gain, preferring the welfare of others to personal satisfaction, and not personal satisfaction to the welfare of others. Thus, the more you concentrate yourselves on the common welfare rather than on your personal welfare, so much more will you become aware of your personal progress; because in all that is used for occasional necessity, charity which ever remains, must excel. (Rule)

lem. The Acts of the Apostles narrate how the early Christians, touched by the power of the Holy Ghost, were one heart and one soul only. This is the aim of our ideal i.e. the first fragrance! In his Rule, Saint Augustine reminds us that we live together in order to live in harmony, so as to form one heart and one soul only, before God. Therefore, if we are living at Sant'Antimo, it is with the purpose to seek God all together, and not in an individualistic manner. Community life is a part of our DNA.

"Community life means living together, eating together, praying together, thinking together, and also for others. It is an antidote for individualistic tendencies - typical of this century. I don't spend my life solely for myself, but for my brothers. When one of them leaves the community in order to preach the Gospel, my prayer accompanies him.

"So too, living together means living according to the Gospel – a

school of charity, which exerts a constant practise of patience. Too easily one can criticise the difficulties brought forth by family life, or wedded couples, if one has made no experience of 'family life'. It is clear that everything is not so easy! The old saying – *vita communis, maxima penitentiæ* – is true, but this type of penance is very appropriate, because it constrains us to overcome our personal instincts. It teaches us that love consists in giving and in.... forgiving. On a purely human basis, living together can also prove to be enriching, because the elderly convey their wisdom to the young, while these convey their enthusiasm. Living together with five or ten brothers allows more freedom - so much so - that when it is necessary to leave aside one's work, for example, in order to study, another brother can always take one's place.

"I have noticed that frequently the Church concentrates its epochs of reform on re-establishing the communal life for priests. At present, many attempts are being made in many Dioceses not without difficulty - and also failure - notwithstanding the fact that the Gospel had been preached in Europe by communities of priests and monks. It's sufficient to recall to mind the Irish monks of the 6th century."

"What is the reason for this?"

"Simply because a priestly community is a living and tangible example of that union which Christ asks us to live in His Gospel. The people are immediately aware of this."

(65) "Just forgive me if I say that I can't see a great difference between the Regular Canons and the Cistercians, who

I had got to know some time ago. They too live in a community."

"It's a well studied observation. But are there not two fragrances still missing?"

"Quite so, but which ones?"

"Here is the second fragrance: Our community of Regular Canons has become part of the Diocese of Siena. As priests or deacons, we have now become part of the 'presbytery' – the College of Priests - in every respect. In fact, the Clerical Sustenance Institute of Siena gives a monthly allowance to those who have a pastoral assignment. We consider the Bishop of Siena as a 'father', and we, in a certain way, as his 'praying voice'. More exactly, we are priests who pray in his name, and for the pastoral necessities of the Diocese. We go to the meetings organised for the priests, and bring along our pastoral and community experiences. We assist the priests in the nearby parishes where they are unable to cope with all the demands of the faithful. The Cistercian monks do none of this!

66 "And then, the last fragrance is the *cura animarum* i.e. the apostolate. We do not become priests for ourselves, but in order to bring Christ to others. Saint Norbert, our point of reference, retains that the priest is he who speaks to God about mankind, and to mankind, about

God. On arriving in this valley in 1980, everything had to be organised, because we had no Evangelisation programme. We examined the local state of affairs, and with the aid of the Holy Ghost, set out in various directions. A typical aspect of the families of Regular Canons is that they adapt the apostolate to the explicit necessities of the place where they live. Just to cite two examples: The Regular Canons called 'Victorines', founded at the centre of medieval Paris, had given such a remarkable impetus to the university teaching, that it spread throughout the whole of Europe. So too, the Regular Canons of Saint Bernard. I suppose you must have heard about the 'Saint Bernard dogs', that carry a bottle of grappa around the neck. Well, these Regular Canons employed these dogs in order to help the pilgrims who crossed the Alps on the Saint Bernard pass. We don't keep dogs, but only cats, and many Christians! While going down the staircase, you will get a closer view of the different places where we carry out our apostolate."

67 After this long and enlightening spiritual chat, we go down the steep staircase that we had climbed so arduously, and then walk along the upper ambulatory where the light creates a most particular and striking effect, as it penetrates across the seven slits in the wall.

Before descending the spiral staircase, we pass through the last room, without windows, which once connected the monks' dormitory to the church and the cloister.

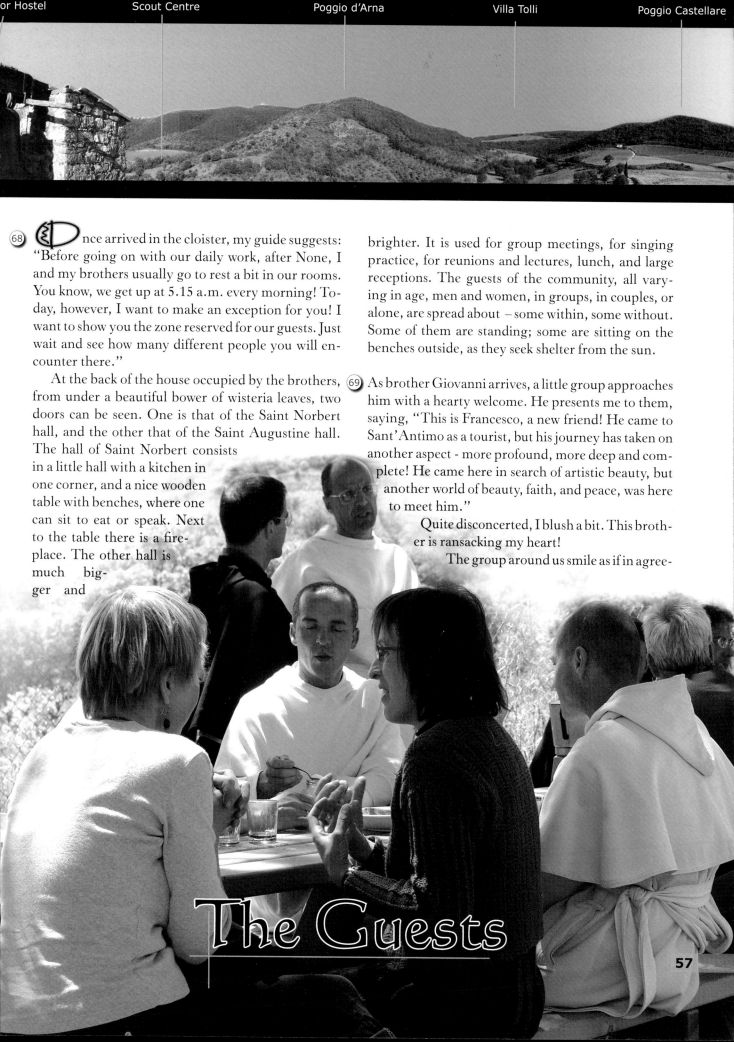

(68) Once arrived in the cloister, my guide suggests: "Before going on with our daily work, after None, I and my brothers usually go to rest a bit in our rooms. You know, we get up at 5.15 a.m. every morning! Today, however, I want to make an exception for you! I want to show you the zone reserved for our guests. Just wait and see how many different people you will encounter there."

At the back of the house occupied by the brothers, from under a beautiful bower of wisteria leaves, two doors can be seen. One is that of the Saint Norbert hall, and the other that of the Saint Augustine hall. The hall of Saint Norbert consists in a little hall with a kitchen in one corner, and a nice wooden table with benches, where one can sit to eat or speak. Next to the table there is a fireplace. The other hall is much bigger and

brighter. It is used for group meetings, for singing practice, for reunions and lectures, lunch, and large receptions. The guests of the community, all varying in age, men and women, in groups, in couples, or alone, are spread about – some within, some without. Some of them are standing; some are sitting on the benches outside, as they seek shelter from the sun.

(69) As brother Giovanni arrives, a little group approaches him with a hearty welcome. He presents me to them, saying, "This is Francesco, a new friend! He came to Sant'Antimo as a tourist, but his journey has taken on another aspect - more profound, more deep and complete! He came here in search of artistic beauty, but another world of beauty, faith, and peace, was here to meet him."

Quite disconcerted, I blush a bit. This brother is ransacking my heart!

The group around us smile as if in agree-

The Guests

ment. Perhaps they too, had been caught up in a similar experience. A lady pulls me aside, and says, "You did very well to come here! There are many things to learn and to do here! One learns how to value silence, how to free oneself from the excess of personal needs, how to give a meaning to one's life, how to enjoy solitude, and at the same time, how to be more charitable towards others. One learns how to pray with one's heart. And then, the brothers are always present! If you need to speak to someone, or want to examine yourself, or need help on a personal or spiritual level, they are constantly at your disposal."

70 In the meantime, two youngsters who are listening with interest, draw near, and one says, "With regard to 'doing' – it is very nice to stay here, because you can also make yourself useful by working, or doing some manual labour. This helps one to understand the value of free service in favour of others. In other words, here it is like a school, where you can learn how to live, while the opportunity to help the brothers presents itself as a very satisfying experience."

"And we are very grateful to you, for all your help," says brother Giovanni, "but we must not forget that this place, first and foremost, is a place dedicated to the praise of God, where prayer is at the centre of everything and pre-

cedes every kind of work. For this reason it is important to work together and to help each other, but it is still more important that one collects one's thoughts in silence, so as to 'hear' and 'welcome' His Presence. Our prayer and our liturgy are undoubtedly an incitement to 'listen' to His voice." We all remain silent for a moment.

One of the girls called Arianna, says, "On account of the friendship between my parents and one of the brothers, I got to know this place when I was still a little child."

Jacopo, a friend of Arianna says, "Since May 2001, I frequent Sant'Antimo."

Arianna goes on to say, "I come here to scan my

THE FOUNDER SAINT NORBERT

Norbert was born at Xanten in Germany, around the year 1080. He died at Magdeburg on the 6th June 1134. His name means 'Prince of the North' or 'Illustrious man of the North'.

He became a subdeacon, and did not advance further. For a while he remained at the service of the Archbishop of Cologne, after which he followed the Emperor Henry V in his entourage. He did not ruin himself by penance. More feasting than prayer - more banquets than fasting. A good example of how a cleric should behave! And at that period, he was not the only one – notwithstanding all the efforts made by popes and bishops to bring about a reform. But one day, in the year 1115, while on a journey, he was almost struck by lightening. This fact shocked him profoundly. Undoubtedly it was certainly a sign, and perhaps also a last warning. He therefore returned to his studies, and once ordained priest he began to travel – always barefooted. He preached to the faithful, but above all to the priests. Before correcting the flock, the shepherd had to be corrected.

In the year 1120 he stopped at Laon in France. From Bishop Bartholemew he obtained an uncultivated valley where he settled down with some clerical companions. And with a plan: the forming of a community of Canons devoted to preaching, and with an exemplary life. In 1121 the Order of Regular Canons was thus founded, and called Premonstratensien – name connected to the valley Prémontré. The discipline was similar to that found in a monastery - community life with work, daily and nightly prayer, but with external preaching adjoined. Thus, a community attached – yes – to the original form of monastic life, but also called to evangelise. Norbert partly anticipated what eventually would have been the mission of the Franciscans, the Dominicans, and other mendicant orders. The white dressed Premonstratensiens so converted the East European population to Christianity – also tilling lands and draining marshes in Holland – as they expanded across the whole of Europe, to venture as far as Palestine (where many were then put to death).

After two centuries characterised by a great expansion (12th and 13th), the time of persecution and abandon drew on – because of religious conflicts in Europe, and the French Revolution. When, in 1834 the General of the Order died without successors, everything seemed to be finished. But in 1839 a new start was made, and today the Premontratensiens are present and active in the Church.

In 1126 Norbert was elected archbishop of Magdeburg, after which they involved him in the dramatic events at the summit of the Church. In the year 1130, after the death of Onorius III, there were two popes at Rome – the pope (Innocent II) and the anti pope (Anaclete II). And the German king Lothair wanted to be crowned at Rome but couldn't distinguish the legitimate pope. Norbert sided with Innocent II (vigorously defended by Bernard), accompanied Lothair to Italy – who knows if he passed by at Sant'Antimo (!) – and intervened so that he was crowned by Innocent II. He continued to be active in Germany, making every effort to restore the Church to unity, and so put an end to the schism.

Norbert died at his Archbishopric See. In 1582 he was canonised by Pope Gregory XIII. At the beginning of 1167 his mortal remains were inhumated in the church of the cenoby of the Premontrarensien Canons at Strahow in the city of Prague, where a magnificent altar was then erected in his honour soon after.

i n -
ner life – that which is more important – because many are the unessential factors that obscure us by their dark shadows. Here on the contrary, we recover what is essential, that which we can fully claim as belonging to us."

Jacopo interrupts, "Here I've found a simple way of life, with a warm and fraternal atmosphere. For me, this is the best place for reflecting and for living an authentic spiritual experience. We also amuse ourselves here, by singing, taking walks, and spending the evenings together, while reunions are held, where we can learn more about real spiritual searching."

Then the brother asks me, "What shall we do now?"

71 My 'personal' guide then suggests, "Let's find a car to take us to the Tabor Hostel." We pass below the house where the brothers stay, while walking along the dirt road that goes to the parking area. On the other side of the main gate, a car driven by one of the brothers is about to leave. We stop him, and the brother says, "I want to show the Tabor Hostel to our visitor. Can you give us a lift up to town?"

The brother at the wheel has a nice face, and a contagious smile. He seems to be in a hurry. He has to go for confessions in a nearby town. While driving along to Castelnuovo dell'Abate, the two brothers talk about the commitments of the community. In the parishes of Castelnuovo dell'Abate, and the neighbouring countryside, all the priests of Sant'Antimo are available for pastoral services i.e. to say Mass, to hear confessions, for baptisms, and funerals etc.

They also tell me about a brother who left by plane some days ago, to preach abroad.

A question regarding the financial aspect crosses my mind. "But who pays all these voyages?"

"As already explained, the Regular Canon lives by his apostolate, unlike other religious orders such as monks or friars who depend on manual labour or mendicity, to earn their living."

72 We have almost arrived at the hostel. For some time now, an incisive question occupies my thoughts. These priests are quite similar to me, young, nice, intelligent, and extroverted. What mysterious force could have impelled them to leave everything – family, friends, and homeland - in order to come and stay here? Which was the voice – and what the words – that could have induced them to reply, 'Yes, I shall go'. I decide to overcome my bashfulness, and quite insolently ask, "But why did you choose to become a priest?"

Pastoral Work

The Call to be a Canon

⑦³ We get out of the car where the steep slope leading to the Tabor hostel begins. After a long silence, the brother who had taken us along with him, says, "It is not so easy to reply to your question. Let's take a short walk, as I try to explain the reason for which I became a priest. Above all, I intend speaking only about my personal experience, which obviously is not the same for every religious. Each vocation in fact, is unique. Each one of us has a personal relationship with God, unlike that of anyone else. And it is also quite difficult to rationalise and to translate into words, that inner, supernatural, insistent and demanding Voice which silently reveals itself with an unheard of, and invincible force, nevertheless tinged with infinite gentleness, as it invites the soul to leave everything in order to follow Him only.

"From a practical point of view, however, things proceeded in a very simple way. I was brought up in a practising Catholic family. As a youth, I frequented the parish, and had a normal life of prayer. I was also a scout. Then, when I was 15 years old, one day, on returning by boat from England, after a holiday of studies, the religious who was guiding our group asked me if I had ever thought about becoming a priest. That question was probably the spark that set aflame the fire already simmering for some time, in my heart. A few minutes after having heard these words, I took my decision - definite and irrevocable – to become a priest."

For a moment the brother stops talking as he fixes his gaze on the far off horizon. I take the opportunity, and intervene, " It is a very moving and enigmatic story. But after having decided to become a priest, why did you choose to live in a community, and precisely in that of the Regular Canons?"

"For three basic motives. The first is because I wanted to share my life with other brothers, rather than live alone as a parish priest. I was very attracted by the Eucharist and I liked the solemn transcendental liturgical chant that elevates the entire celebration to touch such supernal heights. Finally, I wanted to be in midst of the faithful, to care for their souls, and to serve them. These three aspects all united together are found in a community of Regular Canons.

⑦⁴ "My dear Francesco, religious or laymen alike are all called to sanctity, and therefore, you as well; a sanctity that consists in love – loving others as God loves us. For us, following Christ means the realisation of a certain kind of life. Particular observances help us to live the three vows – poverty, consecrated celibacy and obedience – by which we consecrated ourselves to God in a more complete way. These vows are not pledges that end up in themselves, but a specific way by which our manner of life remains constantly orientated towards love.

"The religious formulation of our community holds within it a twofold aspect – contemplative and active life. The liturgy draws us into a particularly deep and personal contemplation of the mystery of Christ, so to nurture the apostolate by what is contemplated, and transmit it to who is out in the world. 'Contemplate to hand over' - two fundamental and inseparable actions of our priestly vocation."

You have allured me, O Lord, and I have let myself be allured. (Jeremias 20,7)

The brother who told me the story of his vocation, greets me and goes off. I voice my thoughts, as I reflect, "Therefore, in your community each one must organise himself in order to contemplate, and for active life."

Brother Giovanni replies, "As for that, we are constantly helped by the regular life. The bell and the liturgical hours constantly set the rhythm of our days, consenting to a well-balanced equilibrium between prayer and occupations – and between an intimate attention to the Voice of God and the preaching of it to the world."

(75) I have yet another question to ask, "What itinerary must be followed, to become a Regular Canon?"

"There are two roads that run along side by side, but nevertheless independent from each other. One road leads to becoming a religious, and the other road leads to becoming a priest. The choice to become a religious does not necessarily include priesthood. In fact, to be a religious signifies the sincere desire to sanctify one's life, to change one's ways, so as to follow Christ as closely as possible. To be a priest, includes all this, as well as the basic desire to serve others. We are priests in order to serve. The term 'religious service' does not exist, while the term 'priestly service' signi-

fies that a priest is ordained for the care of souls and to help his neighbour.

"During the priestly ordination, before receiving the sacred vestments, Saint Norbert put on a simple, woollen tunic. He, who came from an aristocratic family, wanted to demonstrate to everyone present, his intention to unite poverty and a life of penance to the dignity of the priesthood, as Christ his master had done.

"For one who wants to be a religious, the *iter* (journey) begins with the postulation period. After this, about two years of noviceship follow in that place where eventually he hopes to remain. The temporary vows are then taken and last for three years, at the end of which the *iter* concludes with the perpetual profession. The extent of time that passes between the demand to enter the novitiate, and the final religious profession, is absolutely necessary in order to reflect and deepen one's spiritual progress, and to get to know the reality of that communal life to which the religious intends to offer himself entirely. The form pronounced at the moment of the Perpetual Profession adequately expresses the vocation of the Regular Canon, and is as follows: 'I, brother… in offering my person I dedicate myself to the church of Sant'Antimo and promise the

He appointed twelve to remain with Him.
(Mark 3,14)

conversion of my morals and to live the common life of poverty, of consecrated celibacy and obedience according to the Gospel of Christ, the Apostolic See and the Rule of Saint Augustine – in your presence – Bishop of this church, and in the presence of the brothers.' The conversion of morals is specified for every type of religious life, while the specifics of the Regular Canons' priesthood is found in the complete offering of ourselves to the church of Sant'Antimo."

The Tabor Hostel and the Guesthouse

T he brother continues to guide my visit as he explains, "The Tabor Hostel was built recently, and inaugurated in 2000, during the Jubilee year. In order to comply with the environmental protection regulation, it remains almost completely hidden underground, in the hill, below Castelnuovo dell'Abate. In this way the natural landscape remains unspoiled, while in summer the interior remains fresh and cool, and in winter less harsh and severe. It is very suitable for large groups of youngsters. It consists of 4 big apartments, each having a well-equipped kitchen and ample space for dining, as well as showers, bathrooms and large bedrooms, each with 14 beds. Five rooms, each with 3 beds, and also 2 bathrooms, are found in a separate flank where there is another big kitchen and two big halls for reunions. A magnificent view

Tabor Hostel

of the abbey… puts on the finishing touch!

"We also have another place for our guests. It is near the parish church in the town. Until 1992 the community stayed there, but on transferring ourselves to the abbey complex, it has became a guesthouse. It has 10 rooms set out on 2 floors. Most of them have 2 or 3 beds. There are 4 bathrooms. On the ground floor there is a big kitchen, and a spacious dining room. The guesthouse is suitable for couples, families, little groups, and also for single people. I will be expecting you with your family, or your friends."

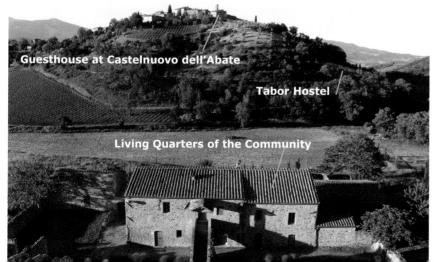

Guesthouse at Castelnuovo dell'Abate

Tabor Hostel

Living Quarters of the Community

We set out, and walk slowly along the road leading to the town. The Starcia valley stretches out to my left, with the abbey at the centre. I stop to have an overall view, and my attention is struck by the various structural and architectonic differences existing between the abbey and the adjacent building. It is evident that the abbey complex has been restored, and I point it out to my friend, the brother, who explains, "When the Papal State rule came to an end in 1870, a sharecropper was living at Sant'Antimo. His presence gave the last glimmer of light that remained. He had made his home in the bishop's apartment, using the Carolingian crypt as a cellar, the church as an agricultural storehouse and the cloister courtyard to keep livestock. That which had been erected by the monks in the 12th century, and that which the bishops had restored in the 15th century, was by then in a pitiful state."

"Don't tell me that such a precious jewel as is this abbey was about to collapse?!"

"Yes, I think that not much was needed to see the entire building crashing down bit by bit. As such, in 1870, when the abbey was put under jurisdiction to the commission of Fine Arts, it still preserved its original 12th century form externally, but there was not a single corner where danger did not threaten. Externally the church was completely surrounded by an embankment with a height that reached up to three meters on the northern side. The roofing was damaged in almost all the various sectors, particularly over the apse, where a speedy intervention was required. Above the south aisle, an additional storey existed, al-most like a loggia, made up of three rooms. Thanks to some sketches made of Sant'Antimo by Ettore Romagnoli in May 1818, we have evidence that a third ambulatory had also existed. All the windows, including the north door, had been stopped up. The absidal section was certainly the most compromised and deteriorated, especially with reference to the decorative elements, such as brackets, columns, capitals and labels. The floor of the nave had been raised. Along the south aisle, for the first three bays, stoppages had been made almost as if to create some separate rooms independent from the rest of the church. These had been built to safeguard the static order and to support the shaky and unsafe arches. In the little central apse, there was an aedicule with ornaments in plaster. Also on the main altar, wooden baroque ornaments were found. All the twin lancet windows above the nave had been walled up. The entire floor of the church was deteriorated for the most part, and the north tribune, without any floor whatsoever."

"You don't say!"

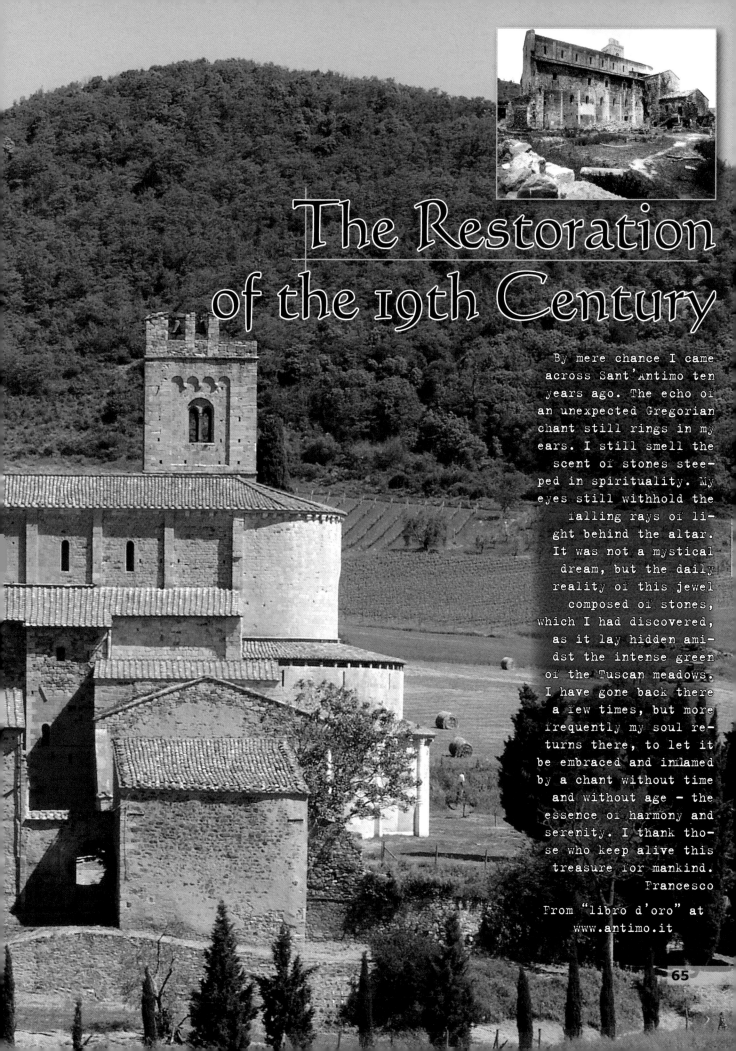

The Restoration of the 19th Century

By mere chance I came across Sant'Antimo ten years ago. The echo of an unexpected Gregorian chant still rings in my ears. I still smell the scent of stones steeped in spirituality. My eyes still withhold the falling rays of light behind the altar. It was not a mystical dream, but the daily reality of this jewel composed of stones, which I had discovered, as it lay hidden amidst the intense green of the Tuscan meadows. I have gone back there a few times, but more frequently my soul returns there, to let it be embraced and inflamed by a chant without time and without age – the essence of harmony and serenity. I thank those who keep alive this treasure for mankind.

Francesco

From "libro d'oro" at www.antimo.it

(78) "No less than seven restoration campaigns were necessary to achieve what we view today. The architect Giuseppe Pantini – a real 'restoration' protagonist - guided the first two: from 1872-1873, and in 1874. He eliminated everything that distorted from the original design. He took away the third ambulatory, the loggia, and some walls built in the nave. He opened the big twin lancet window, lowered the floor of the church, and... very nearly eliminated too the peripheral walls of the tribunes, retaining that they were joined on to the 12th century structure in a latter period. Partini then redrew the church, and used the 'face hammer' abundantly, in order to confer it a regular and old aspect.

He left aside the static sections of the monument, and did not worry about putting in glass panes on the 42 windows of the church; and left a great quantity of sculptured stones outside, which were to finish up in the walls of the neighbouring houses.

"The third campaign made in 1894, proceeded under the directive of the arch. Del Moro. He adjusted the roofing, put in windowpanes, made an intervention in the bell tower, systematized anew the entire floor of the side aisles, and put away the valuable sculptures. His intervention was less marked, but aimed at protecting and preserving the church.

"The fourth restoration campaign was realised by the arch. Moretti, and lasted from 1952-1955. This intervention was also less marked, but indispensable for safeguarding the immobility of the construction. He reinforced and replaced some columns in the zone of the Cabestany capital, where centuries-old underground streams had caused damages of a static kind.

"From 1961-1965, interventions were effected in the chap-

ter hall, and in the ex-refectory, now the actual community house. From 1970-1973, the commission of Fine Arts of Siena remade the entire roof of the church, and renewed almost all the wooden trusses. The façade and the portal were reinforced, and the staircase and floors of the bell tower redone. During that period - also interesting to say - Zeffirelli filmed some scenes here from the life of Saint Francis, for the film entitled "Fratello sole e sorella luna" (Brother Sun and Sister Moon).

"The last campaign, for the moment, dates from 1976-1992 and consisted in minor interventions, more or less in every sector, all aimed at solidifying and protecting the building. From 1988-1992, the community house underwent restoration, so as to let us occupy it on 1st June 1992."

"Quite incredible! More than 100 years were necessary to put Sant'Antimo in order."

"Don't think now that everything is finished. A monument with these dimensions constantly requires attention, and woe betide if the maintenance is omitted only for a few years!"

Veduta dell' esterno del Coro di S. Antimo.

Sketch made in the 19th century by Romagnoli before the elimination of the upper ambulatory and the merlon

To the left: graffiti on the door of the bell tower dating t 1922. Up until 1922 it was still possible to go up to the tribunes.

Walnut stalls designed by the arch. Georgio Cosimi, and executed by the artisan Boris Ciacci. These choir stalls and the sacristy furniture were realised in the year 2000

Economic Activities

My guide has to go off for an appointment, and leaves me to myself. I prefer to return to the abbey, so as to be present at Vespers, because I want to hear once again, the Gregorian chant sung by the community. On making my way to the church, I see a poster indicating a shop that belongs to the abbey – 'L'Arca di Sant'Antimo' (The Ark of Sant'Antimo). I go inside to have a look. The shop assistant, courteous and discreet, permits me to take my time, as I look at all the items on sale. On the walls and the shelves of the cosy little shop, books, pictures, sculptures, marmalade, CDs with Gregorian chant, photos and also hand manufactured articles from other monasteries and con-

L'Arca di Sant'Antimo
Tel: (+39) 0577 835699
E-mail: arca@antimo.it

The Gregorian chant CDs, recorded in the church by the Community, together with the guidebook prove to be a major success. These items are included under the trademark 'Edizioni Sant'Antimo'.

vents, are displayed. The books and CDs realised by the community of Sant'Antimo, are exhibited together with other products bearing the trademark "Edizioni Sant'Antimo." I decide to buy a book and a CD with the chant sung by the brothers. As I leave the shop, I already foretaste the pleasure of sitting on the sofa at home, to listen to, and to enjoy again, the beautiful Gregorian melody that enlivens this place.

The Gregorian Chant

[80] In the book that I have just purchased, I find relevant data on the history of Gregorian chant. Incredible! Quite astounded, I stop along the road going down to the abbey. Since the 4th century, when quite probably the oratory of the martyr Sant'Antimo, had not yet been built, liturgical melodies were already sung. Saint Augustine informs us how Saint Ambrose had composed hymns for the faithful at Milan, roundabout 380. Then, from the 5th-7th century, the repertoire diversifies more or less everywhere. From Visigothic Spain to Gaul, and also in Italy, liturgical repertoires in Latin are invented, to differ not so much in word, as in melody.

It will be Pope Gregory the Great who unites them together, so that henceforth they will be classified by the name 'Gregorian'. The abbey of Sant'Antimo is practically inexistent at that time. When the abbot Tao arrives in the Starcia valley, towards the end of the 8th century, the Gregorian chant is at its apogee. Charlemagne, our 'founder', will partake in spreading the Gregorian chant throughout his empire. In 850, the first musical notation with neumatic writing is invented. In fact, up to this moment, the cantors were accustomed to learn thousands of melodies by heart. Seventy years before the imposing church of Sant'Antimo would be constructed, Guido of Arezzo elaborated a method of musical notation, and sees to its diffusion. The pentagram is thus born, to consist of the notes Ut-Re-Mi-Fa-Sol-La.

Shortly after the construction of Sant'Antimo IV and its completion, the first polyphonies were ringing out under the vaults of Notre Dame in Paris. That the Gregorian chant is so old, and that it had been brought to such perfection in such a remote epoch, really leaves me quite flabbergasted! And at school they teach us that the Middle Ages were a dark period...

These lips shall tell of thy faithfulness, alleluia, to let us sing, alleluia. Gladly these lips will sing of Thee, alleluia. (Psalm 70)

By now, I find myself in front of the church, where I notice a brother walking along slowly with a book in his hand, and a camera hanging around his neck. As I pass by, I hear him softly singing a Gregorian melody. He arouses my curiosity, but I haven't the courage to approach him and question him. The brother perceives my interest, and having stopped singing, he nods to me to come closer. I throw a rapid glance at his camera, and he asks me, "Do you like taking photos?"

"Well, to say the truth… yes. But only so as to amuse myself. I am only an amateur. And you, besides singing, do you like taking photos?"

He gives me a penetrating glance, as he shakes his head, and says, "I use the photos above all for the work connected to the 'Edizioni Sant'Antimo' (Sant'Antimo Editions), with which I occupy myself. In the community I am also in charge of the Gregorian chant."

Gosh! – I think – just the right person from whom to acquire more information on the matter. So I ask, "Could you please tell me something about this old, and also modern type of singing? In fact, I remember that some years ago it was also much in vogue in the discotheques!"

"I prefer not to give a definition of Gregorian chant, because this always proves risky. I would rather like to tell you an interesting little experience I had made when I was studying Gregorian chant at the abbey of Solesmes, in France. This abbey is considered to be a reference point for the world of Gregorian music. As a matter of fact, these Benedictine monks, during the last two centuries brought about its re-birth from where it lay buried under the ashes of the French Revolution. When I chanced to serve the Mass of the choirmaster (who didn't participate at the con-celebration, because he had to conduct the monks' choir), I noticed that at certain moments he interrupted the reading of the text, closed his eyes, and immersed himself in silent meditation. One day, after the Mass, I asked him what did he do during these moments of silence. His reply has forever enlightened me, in understanding the Gregorian chant: 'The Roman Missal proffers only the literary text without music notations, and thus the interpretations are wont to differ. Therefore, while reading the Latin text, I stop in order to recall to memory the music. That which interests me is the Catholic Church's interpretation of the text, and I believe it to be clearly expressed in the Gregorian melody by which the text is imbued."

I am forced to recognise that this brother is speaking about an extraordinarily elevated sphere, for the moment inaccessible to me. Above all, that unpleasant Latin…! "But was it not before the Second Vatican Council of 1960, that the Mass was said in Latin?" I ask.

" Yes, because the rite of Pius V was then in use. After this, the Second Vatican Council actuated a liturgical reform, which drew copiously from the sacred texts of the Old and the New Testaments, in order to restore that primitive aspect which had characterised the religious celebrations at the origins of Christianity. We use this new rite as designated by Paul VI, which prescribes the use of Latin, as the universal language of the Church."

"But what sense can there be in using a dead language?"

"You must understand that no paragon can be made between the profound significance conveyed by the Latin language, and a modern language. For example: In the hymn of the *Benedictus*, found in Lauds, the expression '*Oriens ex alto*' is translated with 'like a dawning on high'. The Latin word does not refer to the sun, but to '*Oriens*' ('orient' – he who rises). By the use of only a single word, various concepts are expressed in Latin. So too, it brings us to understand for example, how the Mass is celebrated while facing Eastwards, because we turn thus towards Him who comes to save us. The liturgical prayer therefore obliges us to 'orientate' also the body. When the term 'dawning' is translated, it los-

The Gregorian chant is born from contemplation and silence.

es the emphasis contained in the words 'Oriens ex alto', because this expression not only refers to rising externally, but also implicates a rising from within. It is something analogous to the light captured, and then released by the alabaster stone in our church, when caught by the sunrays. This is only one example, but I could still furnish many others."

"You know, on thinking carefully, I recall that while listening to the chant, I had perceived a particular richness and powerfulness in the melody, which at this point, I retain should be ascribed to the sonority of the Latin language."

"It is just so. The Gregorian chant, right from the beginning, associates itself with this rich sonority. The Latin language has clothed the Gregorian chant since its beginning, reason for which we chose this language for the sung liturgy. Latin is used in our liturgy also as an example of Ecumenism in the Catholic Church. The Church's universality is very evident at Sant'Antimo, because people come here from all over the world, to listen to the chant. Which language must be chosen in order to receive everyone without distinction between nationality, language or race? Once more the Latin language comes to our aid, because it assembles, and thus unites the whole of mankind in one, just as described in the book of the Apocalypse.

(83) "The chant is not a mere habit or ornament for us. It forms an integral part of our prayer. One prays while singing, and sings while praying. Saint Augustine declares that he who sings, prays twice over (*Enarratio in Psalmos* 72, 1). We consider the Gregorian chant to be an immense treasure, on account of its capacity to draw the soul unto an authentic contemplation of Christ. For this reason we chose to preserve it. The chant creates a resonant musical background to Sacred Scripture, just as the capital of Daniel in the lion's den is a figurative commentary to the word of God. It is as if the melodies which accompany the Eucharist and the liturgical hours- sung from three to four hours daily, 365 days in a year – reveal the silent pulsation of the heart of Jesus."

I remain ever more amazed. His explanations open up anoth-

During the singing lessons of *Vox Christi*
Inf.: emanuele@antimo.it

er world to me. "I begin to understand. A receptive attitude is necessary in order to enter into your liturgy. I imagined that some knowledge of the music technique would suffice to chant the melody. Instead I now come to realise how chanting does not consist so much in doing or in saying, but that it is something essentially more refined and profound. It's a preparation that opens up the soul to receive – the capacity to listen to, and to receive the sound, the word, the chant – because God's Voice speaks through the melody. The reality of the spirit has no need of instruments, but of a voice that sings with an attentive ear. But I want to ask a question - don't you ever make mistakes, or sing some wrong note?"

The brother cantor smiles a bit, and replies, "And quite frequently. You know none of us came here to be a singer. First and foremost, we are here for God, and then we engage ourselves in singing according to our capability. Some of us are more gifted, and others less gifted. It is the heart's attitude, that is important, and not the aesthetic perfection. Saint Augustine well knew that singing is a characteristic of love."

"I see that an enormous heritage is attached to your prayer. But do you also transmit it to others? Do you give lessons on Gregorian chant?"

"For some years now, we organise singing lessons – formally named *"Vox Christi"*. These lessons are in relation to the Liturgy, but we don't concentrate exclusively on Gregorian chant. If you want more information, I suggest you visit our web site." All these explanations leave me quite speechless. They are certainly more than I ever expected. The brother then greets me, as I stand quite dumbfounded at the entrance of the abbey.

A CHANT – CONSECRATED

The Gregorian Chant contains all the norms that characterise a religious consecration: it is a poor, chaste, and obedient chant.

It is a poor chant. Very little is necessary to realise how limited and unpretentious its technical equipment is. But this poverty, in conformity to the Gospel teaching, has nothing to do with indigence. The Gregorian Chant does not lack anything. It is not insipid or inexpressive, but always retains a simple, flexible linearity, free in progression and vivacious in movement, aiming at what is essential, and detached from what is superfluous, also when it has a rich ornamentation.

It is a chaste chant. This is evidenced by its capacity to shun every form of coquetry that could attract attention to itself, of sensuality even subdued, and every form of sentimentalism and mannerism in the means of expression, notwithstanding the rich sensitive qualities. When human feelings are expressed, as often occurs (love, fear, hope, trust, courage, sadness, tiredness, etc.) the Gregorian Chant – as if under a spell – cancels the passionate aspects with their independence and subjectivity to present them calmed down, in order, and dominated by the immensity of divine peace. All this, needless to say, on condition that who interprets the music is also ready to play the game; that he has knowledge of the spirit that animates the work which he intends to express. To see God, and let Him be seen by others, is a privilege conceded only to the pure of heart.

It is an obedient chant. This is most probably the most positive aspect present in the composition of Gregorian Chant. The poor technical equipment and the modesty of expression are to be considered only as preparatory. Along the road of renunciation, the essential is still lacking. The most drastic sacrifice that the Church can demand music to make if it must prove itself worthy of trust, is that it be only music - to accept only a secondary role in serving the liturgical text. The Gregorian melodies do not exist for themselves. By means of an extraordinary docility where freshness and spontaneity remain always intact, they subdue themselves, as a fact, to the text. This does not signify that the melodies remain suffocated, but that frequently they draw prompt inspiration from the text, to form a unity comparable to that of the body and the soul. The melody therefore becomes obedient to the Word of God.

Vespers

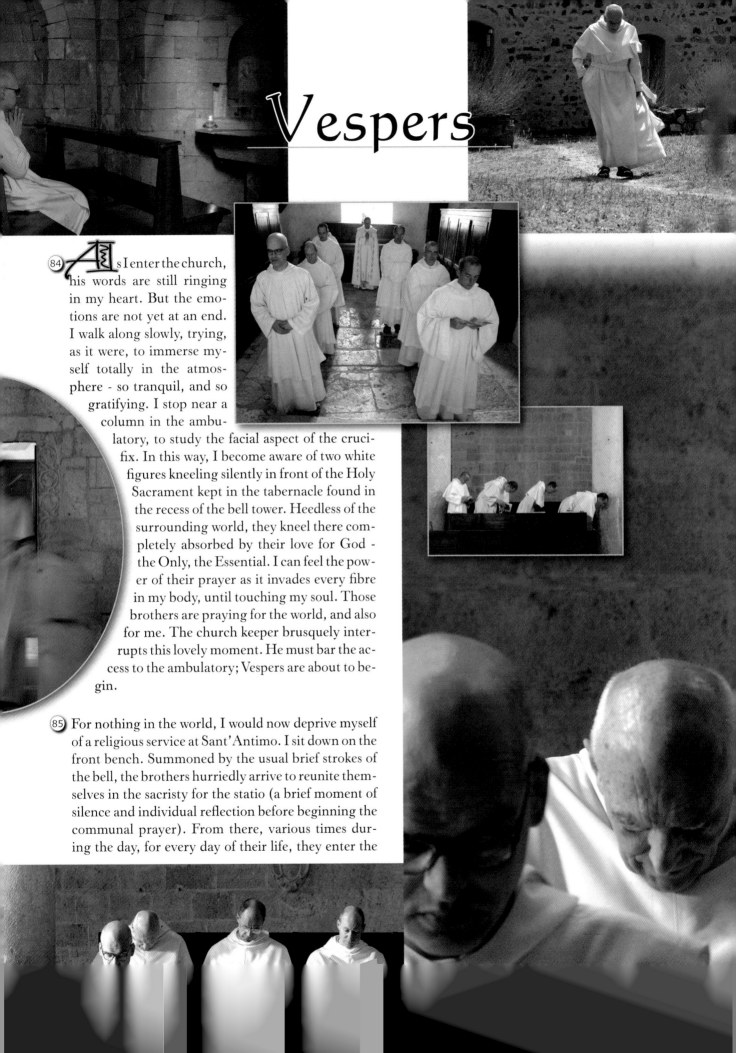

(84) As I enter the church, his words are still ringing in my heart. But the emotions are not yet at an end. I walk along slowly, trying, as it were, to immerse myself totally in the atmosphere - so tranquil, and so gratifying. I stop near a column in the ambulatory, to study the facial aspect of the crucifix. In this way, I become aware of two white figures kneeling silently in front of the Holy Sacrament kept in the tabernacle found in the recess of the bell tower. Heedless of the surrounding world, they kneel there completely absorbed by their love for God - the Only, the Essential. I can feel the power of their prayer as it invades every fibre in my body, until touching my soul. Those brothers are praying for the world, and also for me. The church keeper brusquely interrupts this lovely moment. He must bar the access to the ambulatory; Vespers are about to begin.

(85) For nothing in the world, I would now deprive myself of a religious service at Sant'Antimo. I sit down on the front bench. Summoned by the usual brief strokes of the bell, the brothers hurriedly arrive to reunite themselves in the sacristy for the statio (a brief moment of silence and individual reflection before beginning the communal prayer). From there, various times during the day, for every day of their life, they enter the

church in procession before the sung liturgy.

Vespers is the evening prayer of thanksgiving. It is a moment of intimacy with God - a moment enveloped and emphasised by the fading daylight. Chanting, prayer and light are still marvellously composed in one, just like at Lauds in the early morning, when the rays of the rising sun donate joy and warmth to the chant. The most awesome moment during Vespers is undoubtedly when the brothers intone the *Magnificat* in two alternate choirs. This prayer unites all the Christians to their heavenly mother, Mary, while praising God. 'My soul magnifies the Lord... because He has looked graciously upon the lowliness of His handmaid'.

Vespers is over. The brothers have left the church, to go to supper. The faithful have also left the church. The abbey remains empty and silent, while the last traces of daylight slowly dissolve into darkness.

Dear everyone,

I thank you with all my heart
for the pleasant hospitality
offered me. I really
enjoyed it very much. As
the days go by, I have much
joy in recalling to mind
the lovely moments spent in
prayer, solitude and friendship at Sant'Antimo. You and
Sant'Antimo possess a rich
spiritual endowment where
by many youngsters who are
trying to give a sense to
their life, remain enlightened. This is also an endowment for the Church, not
always so capable of being a
'fount of living water'. I
like to imagine Sant'Antimo
in the future as a community always progressing in its
incessant search for the face
of the Lord, ever athirst
for His love. And with many
new vocations who enliven,
by the silence and peace in
their hearts, those splendid stones and gently slo-
ping hills. This is, and what
Sant'Antimo must be: a coloured rainbow, a setting sun,
a gleaming star, a blooming
flower, a sweet melody, an ear
of wheat, a refreshing
breeze, a fountain where
thirst is quenched, a fertile
land, a warming flame...
Marco (Assisi)

From: "libro d'oro"
at www.antimo.it

74

The Scout Centre

86 I leave the church as the sun is setting. My heart is filled with a profound happiness, up to now unknown to me, and which I want to keep. I walk along the valley, absorbed in my thoughts. As well as the asphalt road that leads from Tabor to the abbey, there's also a footpath hidden by the trees, and which passes across the fields. It lies below the church, and crosses the little tributary of the Starcia, called Colombaiolo, to come up exactly in front of the Tabor Hostel, after having ramped up to the asphalt road that leads to Sant'Angelo in Colle. As I'm walking along the path

surrounded here and there by scout tents, and enlivened by their shouts and songs, a brother comes towards me. He looks me straight in the face and asks me if I'm searching for someone.

"No," I reply, "I'm just taking a walk."

His expression tells me that I have aroused his curiosity. "Are you a boy-scout?" "No, I have never made a similar experience."

"But..." I adjoin as I look about, "perhaps I have missed an important occasion! It seems to me that these youngsters are very lucky. This place with this community is offering them a magnificent opportunity for personal development. I hope they appreciate it."

87 The brother's eyes light up as he says, "You

seem quite a smart chap. Come, now I will show you the Sant'Antimo Scout Centre. As you can see it is situated completely amidst the green. Here, in this field, under the big oak tree, in this little 'baita' in wood, is the reception centre. On the further side of the Colombaiolo stream, where the ample clearings are shadowed over by olive trees, the tents are pitched. Somewhat higher up, the toilet block and a tool depository can be seen. Quite nice, isn't it?"

"It's quite difficult to find something here which is unappealing! But can you tell me when and why the idea of a Scout Centre was born?"

"Most willingly. It was born in 1986, in response to the demands made by big numbers of scout groups in search of a significant and also spiritual place. At the beginning we organised only the reception, with adequate incitements to help the young scouts in choosing a correct direction in their lives, and to help them also in their human, as well as Christian progress. As time went on, the initial proposal was changed, in order to integrate new initiatives, such as the Easter itinerary, the summer route, the Christmas camp, days of spirituality, encounters with youngsters, etc... The Scout Centre aims at offering a deep and in-

tense message, plain and clear, to the many youngsters in search of those important values that give a sense to life. The proposal is prophetic, and uses all the beautiful aspects found at Sant'Antimo, to tend the youngsters towards Christ. The Scout Centre however, is not static. Its future depends on a constant willingness to accept developments, and in keeping pace with the needs of the youngsters. My dear Francesco, no one can ever know what harbours in the hearts of the youngsters that pass by here, but I know for sure that the contact with Sant'Antimo marks each one of them profoundly. I hope that this will avail for you as well."

I like this priest's enthusiasm. One can see how he loves the work he's doing, while his words transmit this love and draw you into it.

The Scout Centre of Sant'Antimo
Tel: (+39) 0577 835550 - E-mail: stefano@antimo.it

The Founding Fathers
of the Community

"But why did the Scout Centre have to be established exactly at Sant'Antimo?"

"Well, let's say that in a certain way the DNA of our community is also Scout! As a matter of fact, Father Andrea and the other founders of the community originally belonged to a group of Scouts named 'The Scouts of Caen', in Normandy, founded in 1969. It 'donated' 10 priestly vocations to the Church. Some of them remained in the Diocese as priests, while another 3, together with their spiritual assistant, Father Andrea, dared to set up a community of Regular Canons. At that time Sant'Antimo was already in a state of abandon for more than 530 years! The Bishop of Siena, Mgr. Ismaele Castellano was thus searching for some religious brothers to give it a new spiritual impact. The assistant Bishop of Siena (ex Bishop of the Laos Missions), was entrusted with the task of encountering us. For us, this was a sign of Providence, because the church where we now carry out our priestly service was thus committed to us.

"We arrived here in October 1979 - a real adventure - but on account of a sound scout experience attained, nothing was able to frighten us! On 8th December 1979, precisely at Sant'Antimo, the community was instituted. Useless to say, the place was not in the same condition as one sees it today! A lot of patience and much work were necessary, before it was possible to settle down in the actual convent. We roamed about for 12 years. First we stayed at Montalcino, then at Vignoni (at San Quirico d'Orcia) and finally at Castelnuovo dell'Abate. Only in the year 1992 did we enter our new dwelling place next to the church. After this, a great deal of work was necessary to put the church and the surroundings into order. The manual labour of an immense number of Scouts played a very important role in this, as they lent us their hands and also their hearts."

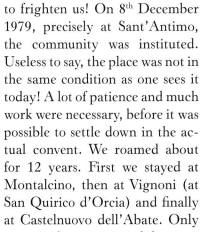

Sant'Antimo 8th December 1979. Clothing ceremony of the first three young men from Normandy. Olivero and Alan are on the right of the Bishop Mgr. Saccioli, and Father Andrea and Stephen, on the left. These last two are still in the Community.

89 The brother greets me and hurries off while the bell is ringing for Compline, the last prayer of the day. I also hurry along. I want to be present right from the beginning. The church is more or less empty. Once again, I sit down on the front bench. Precisely at 8.30 p.m., from the semi-darkness which pervades the side aisle, the white-garbed figures slowly emerge, to advance towards the lit-up presbytery, almost as if in a stage scene. Once again, a strong emotion sweeps over me. The chant begins – slow, calm, almost as if spoken…

Only the voices of the brothers at prayer break the almost surrealistic silence of the church. The atmosphere that reigns, so rich and beautiful, is certainly the most suggestive that I have ever experienced. '*Salva nos Domine, vigilantes, custodi nos dormientes, ut vigilemus cum Christo et requiescamus in pace.*' This is the antiphon of the *Nunc dimittis* recited in Latin. I too manage to understand it. This melody, so gentle, donates peace and tranquillity, as also a tender conviction that one will not be abandoned during the night.

As a final act of this liturgical prayer, a brother blesses the community and all those present, with holy water.

90 A subdued whispering is perceived, as everyone leaves the church. The lights are put out. Only silence reigns. But it is an unusual type of silence, enriched by various sounds – the singing of the crickets and the nightingales! The many voices of nature penetrate the walls of the church, to join the chant of the stones of Sant'Antimo. In silent prayer the brothers confide with their heavenly Mother as they say the rosary while kneeling on the bare floor, or on the kneeling stools. After a day constantly signed by the liturgical hours, and after the final prayer of the day, these priests still desire to be rapt up in God…

While the brothers are in the church, the doors remain open. I don't want to leave the church. I sense a peace that reigns supreme.

91 Strange to say, the church is empty, but I don't feel alone. An intangible presence prevails within the walls of this church. I don't hear any sound, but there is a silence that speaks – the silence of peace, with harmony for its voice. Here all is so perfect, so unique, so unusual, and essential. Here, art, history, beauty, nature, singing, prayer, and faith are found. Here man is found - and God.

Outside,
around Sant'Antimo,
the fields are aglow with fireflies.

Compline

*Would God grant you
to observe all this with love,
enraptured as it were by
the beauty of the spirit,
so that the good fragrance of Christ
be spread by the virtue
of common life.
Not like slaves constrained
to submit to the law,
but like free men under
the action of grace.
(Rule)*

Some Information

RELIGIOUS SERVICES AND VISITING HOURS

Weekdays [1]		Sundays and Holidays [2]	
Matins	5.45 a.m.	Sunday Vigil (* July - August)	12.00 a.m. (* 1.00 a.m.)
Lauds	7.00 a.m.	Lauds	7.30 a.m.
Terce	9.00 a.m.	Terce	9.00 a.m.
Holy Mass	9.15 a.m.	Holy Mass	9.15 - 10.45 a.m.
Visits to church	10.15 a.m. - 12.30 p.m.	Visits to church	11.00 a.m.
Sext	12.45 p.m.	Sext	12.45 p.m.
Lunch	1.00 p.m.	Lunch	1.00 p.m.
None	2.45 p.m.	None	2.45 p.m.
Visits to church	3.00 - 6.30 p.m.	Visits to church	3.00 - 6.00 p.m.
Vespers	7.00 p.m.	Vespers	6.30 p.m. [3]
Supper	7.30 p.m.	Supper	7.15 p.m.
Compline (4 July - August)	8.30 p.m. (4 9.00 p.m.)	Compline (4 July - August)	8.30 p.m. (4 9.00 p.m.)

The above timetable is wont to vary on certain occasions (above all at Christmas and Easter). Consult the abbey's web site.
[1] On certain days Holy Mass is celebrated at 9.30 a.m.
[2] Religious holidays: 1st January – 6th January – 11th May – 15th August - 1st November – 8th December – 25th December.
[3] Followed by the Holy Eucharist Benediction.

NOTICE TO VISITORS

- The church remains open **from 6.00 a.m. to 9.00 p.m.**
- **No payment is required** to visit the church.
- **Visits are not permitted during religious services.**
- While visiting the church:
  You must not disturb the **silence.**
  You must be **dressed decently.**
  You must **switch off the mobile phone.**
- Who desires to have a guided visit can **apply to the church keeper**, always present in the church during visiting hours. Booking is not necessary for groups.
- **Zones of Abbey where visits are permitted:**
  - **Exterior:** can be visited at all hours of the day and night (the abbey is furnished with nightly illuminations until 11.00 p.m.).
  - **Interior:** visits to the nave and side aisles, the ambulatory and crypt under the main altar, are restricted to pre established hours – consult timetable.
- **Zones of Abbey NOT accessible to visitors:**
  - **Exterior:** the cloister (visible from the church entrance), the chapter hall, the Community house, the library, the Carolingian crypt.
  - **Interior:** the Carolingian chapel (sacristy), the tribunes (matroneum).

CONTACT US: Abbazia di sant'Antimo - 53020 Castelnuovo dell'Abate - SI

	Telephone	Fax	E-Mail
Community	(+39) 0577 835659	(+39) 0577 835603	abbazia@antimo.it
Guest house	(+39) 0577 835659	(+39) 0577 835603	foresterie@antimo.it
Scout Centre	(+39) 0577 835550	(+39) 0577 835550	stefano@antimo.it
L'Arca di Sant'Antimo	(+39) 0577 835699	(+39) 0577 835699	arca@antimo.it
Edizioni Sant'Antimo	(+39) 0577 835659	(+39) 0577 835603	edizioni@antimo.it

You will find much more information on visiting our regularly up-dated web site,

www.antimo.it

A Stone that Sings
... and a brother narrates

First edition: march 1993
First reprint: june 1995
Second edition: april 2001
Third edition: july 2004

History did not hand down to us the names of the workmen who had constructed and embellished the abbey. So too, the authors of this guide have chosen to work only for the Glory of God, and for the love of Sant'Antimo, without conveying their names.

Printed in Italy for 'Edizioni Sant'Antimo' by Nuovagrafica - Carpi Tel (+39) 059 691118

July 2005